Personal Choices and Public Commitments

Perspectives on the Medical Humanities

Personal Choices and Public Commitments

Perspectives on the Medical Humanities

Edited by
William J. Winslade

Institute for the Medical Humanities
Galveston, Texas

Texas Committee for the Humanities
Austin, Texas

Library of Congress Cataloging-in-Publication Data

Personal choices and public commitments: perspectives on the
 the medical humanities / edited by William J. Winslade.
     p.   cm.
    Bibliography: p.
    ISBN 0-9621294-0-2
    1. Medical ethics. 2. Humanism. I. Winslade, William J.
II. University of Texas Medical Branch at Galveston. Institute for the
Medical Humanities. III. Texas Committee for the Humanities.
    [DNLM: 1. Ethics, Medical. 2. Humanism. W 50 P467]
R724.P43 1988
174'.2—dc19
DNLM/DLC
for Library of Congress   88-38861
                               CIP

We gratefully acknowledge the following people and publishers for permission
to reprint copyrighted material:
    Albert J. Jonsen, "What Does Life Support Support?" Copyright © 1987 by
ALPHA OMEGA ALPHA HONOR MEDICAL SOCIETY, reprinted by permission from THE PHAROS, Volume 50, Number 1.
    Sally A. Gadow, "Death and Age: A Natural Connection?" Copyright © 1987
by *Generations*, 833 Market St., Suite 516, San Francisco, California 94103. Reprinted by permission.
    Vassar Miller: The poems "Introduction to a Poetry Reading," "On the
Examination Table," and "Spastics" ("First poem from Handi-Lib"), in *If I Could
Sleep Deeply Enough,* are reprinted by permission of Vassar Miller.

Institute for the Medical Humanities
The University of Texas Medical Branch
Galveston, Texas 77550

Contents

Foreword   vii
Melvyn H. Schreiber

Preface and acknowledgments   ix

Contributors   xi

Introduction   xiii

Essays

1. **Literature and Medicine: Illness from the Patient's Point of View**   1
   Anne Hudson Jones

2. **Life History, Oral History, and Case History: The Story of Eldrewey Stearns, Integration Leader**   16
   Thomas R. Cole

3. **"Babe" Didrikson Zaharias: Her Personal and Public Battle with Cancer**   33
   Susan E. Cayleff

4. **Caring for Congenitally Handicapped Newborns**   47
   Ronald A. Carson

5. **What Does Life Support Support?**   61
   Albert R. Jonsen

6. **Life and Death Choices: The Patient's Rights**   70
   William J. Winslade

7. **Death with Dignity: Patients' Rights and the Texas Hospice Movement**   81
   Rebecca Dresser

8. **Death and Age: A Natural Connection?**   93
   Sally A. Gadow

9. **In Whose Image? Ethical Issues in Genetic Engineering**   101
   Thomas H. Murray

v

10. **A Glimpse at Galveston's Medical Past, 1836–1885**   114
   Chester R. Burns

11. **Abortion in Texas: Legal Enactments, Religious Traditions, and Social Hegemony**   129
   Harold Y. Vanderpool

Lectures and participants   148

Texas medical humanists   151

Selected bibliography   163

Foreword

Never before have technological advances in medicine been so numerous and impressive or occurred at such a rapid rate. As a radiologist, I am particularly aware of the numerous and often technologically complex examinations available for the diagnosis and care of patients. While in times past, a history and physical examination might be supported by an occasional x-ray study, today we have at our command the use of such extraordinary devices as computerized body tomography, color doppler ultrasound, dual photon absorptiometry, magnetic resonance imaging, and a large array of innovative interventional procedures for therapy.

The availability of this abundance of diagnostic and therapeutic treasures brings with it a subtle but pervasive danger: that we will so concentrate on what is wrong with the patient's body that we may fail to recognize fully that it is a whole patient with whom we deal, a human being with fears, hopes, needs, and expectations.

It is the job of humanists everywhere and medical humanists in particular to emphasize the importance of human values in medicine, even when difficult problems and ambiguous data make it tempting to apply rules and procedures that simplify decisions but that may not properly attend to human needs and concerns and that may, in the end, not be particularly humane.

The authors of the essays in this volume have emphasized the importance of attention to the needs of persons as well as to the needs in people. Anne Jones comments that "one reason for the increase in patient-authored narratives in the United States is that people's innate need for autonomy and control over their lives is challenged by serious or terminal illness. And when this already threatening situation is exacerbated by the dehumanizing technological environment of the modern hospital and contemporary medical treatments, the need to have some control and to find some meaning in the experience becomes even greater." She goes on to describe the use of literature in medicine, and she tells about having students in the health sciences "imagine themselves in the patient's role so that their attention shifts from their own needs to those of the patients. . . . The goal is empathy, the basis for any truly ethical medical practice." Her essay reminds us that "to the age-old fear of suffering serious injury or illness, we now have added the peculiarly contemporary fear of becoming a victim of sophisticated medical technology, whose 'miracles' can prolong the impaired lives and suffering of people, sometimes against their will."

In Ron Carson's essay on caring for congenitally handicapped newborns, he speaks of medicine's mistrust of emotion, the presumption being that strong feeling muddles the mind, that emotions are unruly and that thinking is orderly. He offers a challenge: ". . . to find a way to include such feelings by giving them form. Feeling, given articulate form, can inform action." Medicine is not merely the application of scientific principles to the care of the sick. Doing it right requires insight into and understanding of the emotions and feelings of both the patient and the healer, and Carson argues that this is not merely an important but an essential element in comprehension and ultimately in decision making.

Bill Winslade, who edited this volume, discusses legal options and patients' rights regarding life and death choices. "The law permits and encourages the difficult but significant conversations about patients' preferences concerning the use of life-support technologies. Only if such conversations do occur can respect for patients' choices be realized; if desires are not stated and not clarified we will never know how to show appropriate respect for the unique human capacity to make self-conscious choices about values and preferences, especially the uniquely personal choices that some can make about their own death and dying."

These and the other essays in this splendid collection discuss those things that humanists and that which is humane in each of us seek to enlarge and improve: respect for patients as persons and for the informed choices they make for themselves. It is the application of that principle that enables us to design public commitments that serve personal choices.

Melvyn H. Schreiber, M.D.

Preface and acknowledgements

In order to increase public understanding of recent contributions made by scholars in the humanities to difficult issues in medicine, the Institute for the Medical Humanities at the University of Texas Medical Branch at Galveston, with the support of a $14,775 grant from the Texas Committee for the Humanities (a state program of the National Endowment for the Humanities), sponsored a series of public lectures and discussions in ten Texas cities (Beaumont, Corpus Christi, Denton, Edinburgh, Fort Worth, Galveston, Georgetown, Lubbock, Nacogdoches, and San Angelo). The success of the series prompted us to make the lectures (revised for a reading audience) available to a wider public and professional audience. We are grateful to Judith Wilson Ross and Anne Donchin for their critiques of the text.

In each of the cities we visited, a local coordinator helped to identify discussants, to find a site for the lecture, to notify the local media, and to assist with numerous necessary details of local arrangements. We owe special thanks to Barbara Carr, Elizabeth Erkel, Pete A. Y. Gunter, Rumaldo Juarez, Ted Klein, Tom McGovern, G. Benjamin Oliver, Jo Anne Stiles, and Judithe Hanover Zenter. In addition, moderators and discussants from the local communities and universities (listed on pages 152-54) added their insights and comments to the lecture presentations. We appreciate very much their interest and participation.

After the lectures stimulated considerable local and statewide interest, we decided that a Directory of Texas Medical Humanists would be of value to the general public, scholars, hospitals, librarians, and others. The Directory is included on pages 155-66.

The staff of the Texas Committee for the Humanities was extremely cooperative and helpful in every phase of our project. Special attention to our project from Kathleen Capels, Gregory Jones, and James Veninga enabled us to manage administrative matters effectively.

The Advisory Board for the project provided valuable guidance during the initial phase of the project. The members of the Advisory Board were Chester R. Burns, Frances Harris, Lewis Harris, Julian Kitay, Ted Klein, Toby Mattox, G. Benjamin Oliver, and Mike Tolson.

We are also deeply indebted to the diligent efforts of the editorial, administrative, and secretarial staff of the Institute for the Medical Humanities for their role in bringing this project to fruition. Lucy Enriquez helped to coordinate the lectures and the press releases; Kathy Stephens edited and organized the manuscript for publication; Donna Polisar assisted in identifying Texas medical humanists and helped with bibliographical research; Cielo Perdomo prepared the Directory of Texas Medical Humanists; Betty Herman not only kept track of the numerous documents that the editor regularly misplaced, but also made sure, with the assistance of other

Institute secretaries, that all the essays were properly prepared for publication; Beverly DeVries managed effectively the innumerable bureacratic and administrative details of grant administration. It is a great pleasure to be a part of and work with such a congenial group of colleagues.

Contributors

Chester R. Burns, M.D., Ph.D., is James Wade Rockwell Professor of Medical History in the Institute for the Medical Humanities, The University of Texas Medical Branch at Galveston (UTMB).

Ronald A. Carson, Ph.D., is Kempner Professor and director of the Institute for the Medical Humanities, UTMB.

Susan E. Cayleff, Ph.D., is associate professor of women's studies, San Diego State University.

Thomas R. Cole, Ph.D., is associate professor of history and medicine in the Institute for the Medical Humanities, UTMB.

Rebecca Dresser, J.D., is associate professor in the School of Law and the Center for Biomedical Ethics, School of Medicine, Case Western Reserve University.

Sally A. Gadow, Ph.D., is associate professor of philosophy in the Institute for the Medical Humanities, UTMB.

Anne Hudson Jones, Ph.D., is associate professor of literature and medicine in the Institute for the Medical Humanities, UTMB.

Albert R. Jonsen, Ph.D., is professor of ethics in medicine and chairman of the department of medical history and ethics at the School of Medicine, University of Washington.

Thomas H. Murray, Ph.D., is director of the Center for Biomedical Ethics, School of Medicine, Case Western Reserve University.

Harold Y. Vanderpool, Ph.D., is professor of the history and philosophy of medicine in the Institute for the Medical Humanities, UTMB.

William J. Winslade, Ph.D., J.D., is professor of medical jurisprudence and psychiatry in the Institute for the Medical Humanities, UTMB.

Introduction

These essays present the views of scholars of literature, history, theology, philosophy, and jurisprudence who concentrate their research on the humanities in medicine. The essays are written for general audiences similar to those that heard the original lectures. Although some of the essays may be of particular interest to Texans, each of them addresses issues of wider public and professional concern.

The first three essays in this collection examine illness and suffering from the point of view of the individual patient. Illness and suffering both fascinate and frighten us. We know humans are vulnerable, finite creatures who are born, live, and die. Some suffer and die; others suffer and survive—for a time. From those who suffer we learn about their lives and perhaps about our own. We identify with those who are ill because we are all vulnerable. Yet we also want to distance ourselves from illness and suffering; we want to understand it and yet we are repelled by it because we fear for ourselves. Several of the lectures in this collection call our attention to illness and suffering of particular persons in life as well as literature. From these narratives we may gain insight and understanding. And we may catch glimpses of the meaning of the human condition. This is one dimension of what have come to be known as the medical humanities.

Sometimes the medical humanities concern the illness and suffering not only of particular individuals, but also of categories of persons, such as handicapped newborns or the terminally ill. Several essays explore patterns of illness and suffering and our limited but sincere efforts to come to terms with the context, values, choices, and consequences of illness, disability, dying, and death. These are perhaps the most familiar and yet intractable issues in the medical humanities. Thus it is not surprising that several essays attempt to explain, clarify, and interpret aspects of illness, suffering, and death that are increasingly prominent features of our lives.

Illness and suffering are experienced in the present, but they have been with us in the past and will confront us in the future. Some of the essays examine issues that are of current concern, while others seek insights from the past. Careful attention to historical facts can sometimes yield insights that help us better understand our present situation. And attempts to anticipate the future can enable us to understand as well as cope with choices that await us. Thus several of the essays sketch historical patterns or examine historical facts in detail. Others attempt to clarify current concerns. And still others try to guide us toward an understanding of the future.

The humanities at their best help us to enlarge our vision, sharpen our interpretations, and deepen our understanding. The medical humanities provide ways of seeing and understanding, among other things, illness and suffering. The essays in this collection are perspectives on illness and suffering that offer insights and interpretations that will guide readers to a greater appreciation of our common fate.

Literature and Medicine:
Illness from the Patient's Point of View

Anne Hudson Jones

Illness and suffering—so inescapably a part of the human condition—have been themes of great literature throughout the centuries, going back in the Western tradition at least as far as the Biblical book of Job. In the past decade, the frequency of appearance of literary works dealing with illness, injury, and death has quickened, so much so that in 1979 Mel Gussow, the *New York Times* drama critic, wrote a feature article about the patient as hero in contemporary Broadway plays (such as *Whose Life Is It Anyway?*, *The Shadow Box*, *Wings*, *Nevis Mountain Dew*, *Inacoma*, and *Children of a Lesser God*.)[1] And a new term—"pathography"—has been coined for the hundreds of narrative accounts of illness that have been published in the last two decades (for example, John Gunther's *Death Be Not Proud*, Cornelius Ryan's *A Private Battle*, Norman Cousins's *Anatomy of an Illness*, Martha Lear's *Heartsounds*, etc.). Why this recent spate of works about illness and this shift in focus from doctor-as-hero to patient-as-hero? To the age-old fear of suffering serious injury or illness, we now have added the peculiarly contemporary fear of becoming a victim of sophisticated medical technology, whose "miracles" can prolong the impaired lives and suffering of people, sometimes against their will. The patients' rights movement has come of age, as has handicap lib, and both have found expression in our poetry, plays, novels, and movies. At the same time, a new field known as literature and medicine has been born.

When programs in medical humanities began to emerge in medical schools in the United States fifteen years ago, the first burst of enthusiasm was for medical ethics. In the last five years, however, there has been an increasing interest in literature and medicine. This interest has been encouraged, surprisingly enough, even by several medical ethicists who have turned from traditional analytic philosophy to narrative to help them articulate and demonstrate important values in medicine. These ethicists explain their use of narrative more in terms of the inadequacy of contemporary ethical theory than in terms of the special aesthetic qualities of literary narratives. I want to begin by summarizing some of their concerns to help explain the importance of narrative and literature in the education of physicians and other health care professionals, as well as in our society's discussions of medical ethics.

In their 1977 article "From System to Story: An Alternative Pattern for Rationality in Ethics,"[2] David Burrell and Stanley Hauerwas offer first a detailed critique of the standard account of moral rationality in contemporary ethical theory and then an argument for the significance of narrative for ethical reflection. In their critique, they explain that "contemporary ethical theory has tried to secure for moral judgments an objectivity that would free such judgments from the subjective beliefs, wants, and stories of the agents who make them" (pp. 112-113). This attempt, they argue, has resulted partly from the inspiration of the scientific ideal of objectivity and partly from the assumptions of modern pluralist democratic theory. As they explain: "Many thinkers have tried to free the objectivity of moral reason from narrative by arguing that there are basic moral principles, procedures, or points of view to which a person is logically or conceptually committed when engaged in moral action or judgment" (p. 114). The goal of such attempts is "to provide an account of moral duty that is not subject to any community or tradition" (p. 114), but is "based on rationally derived principles that are not relative to any one set of convictions" (p. 115). As a result, Burrell and Hauerwas argue, contemporary ethics—particularly, contemporary medical ethics in the United States—has become a branch of decision theory. And the underlying assumption that most of our moral concerns—and particularly, our medical ethical concerns—are "'problems'" suggests that "ethics can be construed as a rational science that evaluates alternative 'solutions'" (p. 115).

Burrell and Hauerwas object that "the standard account's project to supply a theory of basic moral principles from which all other principles and actions can be justified or derived represents an attempt to make the moral life take on the characteristics of a system" (p. 121). They argue that the standard account is seriously inadequate as a description of our moral existence because our lives are too richly textured and various to fit such a monochromatic account or system. Let me quote briefly from their argument:

> There can be no normative theory of the moral life that is sufficient to capture the rich texture of the many moral notions we inherit. What we actually possess are various and sometimes conflicting stories that provide us with the skills to use certain moral notions. What we need to develop is the reflective capacity to analyze those stories, so that we better understand how they function. It is not theory-building that develops such a capacity so much as

close attention to the ways our distinctive communities tell
their stories. Furthermore, an analysis of this sort carries us
to the point of assessing the worth these moral notions
have for directing our life-projects and shaping our stories.
(p. 121)

Of their important claims for the significance of narrative in ethical reflection, I want to emphasize two: first, "that character and moral notions only
take on meaning in a narrative" (p. 112); and second, "that narrative and
explanation stand in an intimate relationship, and, therefore, moral disagreements involve rival histories of explanation" (p. 112).

Larry R. Churchill's 1979 essay "The Human Experience of Dying: The
Moral Primacy of Stories over Stages"[3] is a critique of the dominance that
Elisabeth Kübler-Ross's paradigm of the five psychological stages of dying
has attained. Kübler-Ross's work with dying patients revolutionized teaching in the health care professions about death and dying. From interview-
ing hundreds of patients, Kübler-Ross developed her schema of the five
psychological stages—denial, anger, bargaining, depression, and acceptance—that she claims most dying patients experience. Churchill's point is
that the stages have become a normative pattern, a progressivist philosophy, that tempts us—and particularly the health care professionals among
us—to impose the pattern on a dying person. Churchill objects: "When we
become obsessed with these stages as normative protocol we are treating
dying as a technical problem" (p. 26). Churchill argues further that "the
most pernicious aspect of a rigid adherence to the stages is the usurpation
of the dying person's right to speak the meaning of his or her own death"
(p. 28), and he calls for a return to story—an account of incidents or events
in a narrative or dramatic form—as a corrective. Churchill maintains that
"the perceived world has power over the logically-ordered world of the
health sciences" (p. 30), and he concludes that "it is morally incumbent upon
those who care for the dying to reduce their reliance upon stages and instead
listen to stories" (p. 32). Although Churchill focuses on psychological
concepts rather than philosophical principles, his point is similar to the one
made by Burrell and Hauerwas. Human beings and their psychological and
moral experiences do not fit rigid, abstract, rational systems. Applied as
normative imperatives, such systems are immoral because they deny
people the right of interpreting their own experiences—of telling their own
stories.

Robert Coles—psychiatrist, moralist, and literary scholar—tells of having taught courses in medical ethics or moral philosophy that ended with

his certainty that his students had become superb logicians but had not necessarily become more ethical human beings or physicians. He now teaches only literature in his medical humanities course, as he explains in his 1979 article "Medical Ethics and Living a Life."[4] "The point of a medical humanities course devoted to literature," he says, "is ethical reflection, not a bit of culture polish here, a touch of story enjoyment there" (p. 445). In his course he uses novels such as George Eliot's *Middlemarch*, Sinclair Lewis's *Arrowsmith*, F. Scott Fitzgerald's *Tender Is the Night*, and Walker Percy's *Love in the Ruins*. He argues that such novels explore "a kind of medical ethics that has to do with the quality of a lived life" (p. 445). His point is that medical ethics cannot be separate and discrete from one's general moral sensibility. And he calls for teaching a kind of medical ethics that "move[s] us to pursue . . . moral inquiry of a wide-ranging kind, in the tradition of . . . the best of our novelists: intense scrutiny of one's assumptions, one's expectations, one's values, one's life as it is being lived or as one hopes to live it" (p. 446).

Warren Reich, in his 1985 paper "Experiential Ethics as a Foundation for Dialogue between Health Communication and Health-Care Ethics,"[5] defends the principle-based paradigm in medical ethics, especially in the arena of public policy debates, but he also asserts that "principle-based 'quandary ethics,' which today is the dominant paradigm for health-care ethics, is inadequate for ethical reflection on the moral issues in health care" (p. 7). He claims that it is "hazardously incomplete—to define ethics solely in terms of discursive reasoning whereby rational principles incorporating universal moral concepts are applied to moral dilemmas so as to determine deductively what is right and wrong behavior" (p. 7). "Ethics requires a corrective paradigm," he says, "which can be called experiential ethics" (p. 7). He continues: "The focal point of experiential ethics [is] the models and images that guide our moral vision and our moral behavior" (p. 9). Such "models of moral attitude and behavior in medicine are provided," he says, "by *character-images* in stories, myths, and fables; and," he continues, "the story itself may create an *ethos-paradigm* that enables the health professional to revision the value dimension of his or her entire career or professional life" (p. 11). He concludes: "The term 'narrative ethics' can be used to embrace these themes; the methodology is still that of experiential ethics, for narrative presents the world of moral experience to us" (p. 11).

The shortcomings of the traditional principle-based paradigm for medical ethics are clearly delineated in the works of these five ethicists. All five recognize the limits of rationality and logical analysis as a basis for morality, and all turn to narrative as a corrective. Narrative, however, means something different to each of them. For Burrell and Hauerwas, it means communal and religious myths; for Churchill, patients' stories—of the kind that are now being called "pathography"; for Coles, literary novels; and for Reich, a combination of "speech, written word, film, etc., in the form of stories, reports, fables, myths, news accounts, scientific studies, etc." (p. 8).

For my purposes here, I'll focus on narratives of illness presented from the patient's point of view—regardless whether they are autobiographical, biographical, fictional, or poetic in form. My concern is with what I'll call the narrative paradigm for medical ethics. The most important implication of a shift from the principle-based paradigm of medical ethics to a narrative paradigm is the concomitant shift in power. The narrative paradigm is non-hierarchical and assumes that all people have the capacity to be rational.[6] In medical settings, this paradigm would call for patients' narrative control of their own stories.[7]

Historically, the first kind of narrative to become part of clinical medical practice was authored and controlled by physicians, even though it was called the patient's history (or the case history). Medical historians tell us that it was a significant step forward in medical practice when physicians could be persuaded to keep detailed notes of the history and progress of their patients. Since that time, the narrative history has become a standard part of physicians' records in the United States, and courses in many medical schools are devoted to teaching students how to interview patients and take a medical history from them. What is still sometimes called the patient's history, however, is really the history of the illness rather than of the patient. Physicians write these narratives in their own terms, using their own language and disciplinary classification schema. Obviously, physicians record only what they consider to be important, and for most of this century biomedical facts and physiological findings have been considered more clinically significant than psychosocial facts or patients' interpretations of their illnesses.[8] The medical case history is designed for a very limited audience: other physicians (and, increasingly, lawyers). Patients rarely get to read this physician-authored narrative. To gain access to their own case histories, patients may even have to go to court to get a legal order giving them the right to see their medical records.

As dissatisfaction with medical care has grown in the United States during the past two decades, there has been a small redressing of the balance by a spate of narratives written by patients. These have become so frequent that people have begun referring to them as "pathographies"—autobiographical or biographical accounts of an illness. Although pathographies from earlier centuries can be found, they are many fewer in number than those being produced in the United States now. Patients now seem to have a compelling need to tell their stories. Why? I suspect that one reason for the increase in patient-authored narratives in the United States is that people's innate need for autonomy and control over their lives is challenged by serious or terminal illness. And when this already threatening situation is exacerbated by the dehumanizing technological environment of the modern hospital and contemporary medical treatments, the need to have some control and to find some meaning in the experience becomes even greater. The intended audience for these accounts seems to be physicians and other health care professionals as well as other patients or potential patients. Often these accounts are angry, aimed to get physicians to pay attention to the patient's experience, which may not have been important to the physicians who actually treated the patient. In that sense, these works are intended as correctives of abuses within the medical setting. They are narratives for medical ethics, strictly speaking. Other patients' narratives are not angry but reflective, seeking to make meaning of a devastating illness, suffering, or prolonged dying.

If we think of the patient as author of his or her own life story, then the physician's role toward the patient is very different from the paternalistic one physicians have traditionally held toward patients. No longer the author of the patient's story, the physician must give over control to the patient-narrator. This means that physicians must give patients the information they need to choose the appropriate next episode in their stories rather than make choices for the patient. When patients are allowed to make decisions for themselves, physicians' need for skill in quandary ethics is considerably lessened. In narrative ethics, physicians must respect patients' choices for their own lives and stories. There are limits to this narrative paradigm, however. Obviously those patients who are unconscious or mentally incompetent cannot narrate their own stories. Someone else must choose the next episode on their behalf. But even for these patients, the narrative paradigm can be helpful. In trying to choose for someone else, it is important to consider not only biomedical facts but also features of a particular patient's story as far as it has been previously written. The appropriate ending for one patient's story might be entirely inappropriate for another. Here Churchill's argument provides a useful example. The attempt to force all patients to progress through Elisabeth Kübler-Ross's five stages of dying, as if there could be only one right way to die—or stage to die in—is ludicrously oversimplistic and ultimately immoral. One's death should fit one's life if there is to be coherence and meaning in a story. Someone who has always been a fighter may more appropriately die still fighting rather than in passive acceptance, as Dylan Thomas counsels his father to do in his famous poem "Do Not Go Gentle into That Good Night":

> Old age should burn and rave at close of day;
> Rage, rage against the dying of the light.

Churchill calls for physicians to listen to patients' stories. Rita Charon, an internist on the faculty of Columbia University's College of Physicians and Surgeons, goes further. She asks her students to write their patients' stories—not in the format of the traditional medical history (which they do also as part of their expected duties) but from the patient's point of view.[9] And if they don't know the facts about a patient's story, Charon has them make them up. The point is to have students imagine themselves in the patient's role so that their attention shifts from their own needs to those of the patients. For this exercise, the mood and behavior of the patients are more important than missing details about their lives. Point of view is more important than facts. Essentially, Charon has her students write a fictional story about their patients. Like Churchill, she has an ethical end in mind. She wants her students to try to understand the meaning of illness from the point of view of the patient. The goal is empathy, the basis for any truly ethical medical practice, and Charon finds this narrative exercise more helpful than analytic philosophy. She wants her student physicians to be virtuous people, and she hopes that out of virtue they will act ethically. Hers is an empirical experiment; any theory of how narrating another's story leads to increased empathy and perhaps to more ethical medical practice has yet to be fully elaborated. Churchill, Coles, Charon, and Reich are not alone in their search for ways of inculcating empathy and virtue rather than encouraging logical brilliance in decision making. The language of medical education now is increasingly given over to concern about how to produce compassionate, caring healers rather than dispassionate, objective technicians. One way is to have students listen to patients' stories.

The problem that led ethicists to analytic philosophy in the first place, however, is that of judging among competing subjective narratives.[10] Some stories are better than others; some have power and force that others lack. As Genly Ai, Ursula Le Guin's protagonist in *The Left Hand of Darkness*, phrases it: "Truth is a matter of the imagination. The soundest fact may fail or prevail in the style of its telling."[11] And besides, there are literally hundreds and thousands, even hundreds *of* thousands, of patients' stories that one could listen to—and hundreds that one could read. A physician in practice should listen to each and every one of his or her patients' stories. That is clearly what Churchill calls for in his article "The Moral Primacy of Stories over Stages." To do otherwise is to treat the patient as if he or she is not a person. In teaching, however, we need stories that "prevail in the style of [their] telling," stories that reverberate beyond the individual experience of the narrator or author to imply something of universal significance for us all. That is why literature—works shaped by authors of some accomplishment and skill—may be more important in the education of physicians than personal narrative—that is to say, stories told by individual but narratively inexperienced patients. Yet even if we limit ourselves, for reasons of such pedagogical efficiency, to only literary accounts, there are many, many works we could use.

As my literary examples, I have chosen works of two Texas writers, Vassar Miller and Larry McMurtry. McMurtry probably needs no introduction, but Vassar Miller may. She is a native Houstonian and an award-winning poet, nominated for the Pulitzer Prize in 1960. Born in 1924, Miller has suffered from cerebral palsy all her life. She is remarkably gifted and has found a way to speak despite her physical handicap. I'll present three of her poems, because she speaks for a group of people whose voices we rarely hear. "Introduction to a Poetry Reading" opens her volume *If I Could Sleep Deeply Enough*:

> I was born with my mod dress sewn onto my body,
> stitched to my flesh,
> basted into my bones.
> I could never, somehow, take it all off
> to wash the radical dirt out.
> I even carry my own rock
> hard in my mouth,
> grinding it out bit by bit.
> So, bear me
> as I bear you,
> high, in the grace of greeting.[12]

Although Miller is usually categorized as a religous poet, I have selected from her poems two that focus specifically on her experience as a patient and as a disabled person. The first is titled "On the Examination Table":

> My eyes, two birds
> crazily threshing
> in the trap of their sockets,

my tongue, dry leaf
ready to fall
to the pit of my throat,

my breath, fragile moth
caught in a cave-in
of my gullet's tight tunnel,

my belly, overturned turtle,
stripped from the shell
of daily decorum,

my body, dull dog,
shies into terror's
mythical monster.[13]

In this poem, Miller conveys through her vivid metaphors the helplessness of a patient laid out on the examination table. That helplessness is exacerbated in her case by her physical disability, and her metaphors are well chosen to describe her physical condition. But anyone who has been laid out naked on an examination table can recognize and identify with the feelings that she is describing.

Miller says things that the rest of us, that is, those of us who are not physically disabled, may not want to hear. She writes of physically disabled people who are just like the rest of us in their basic human emotions and desires. For example, consider her poem "Spastics," subtitled "(First poem from Handi-Lib)":

They are not beautiful, young, and strong when it strikes,
but wizened in wombs like everyone else,
like monkeys,
like fish,
like worms,
creepy-crawlies from yesterday's rocks
tomorrow will step on.

Hence presidents, and most parents, don't have to worry
No one in congress will die of it. No one else.
Don't worry.
They just

hang on
drooling, stupid from watching too much TV,
born-that-way senile,

rarely marry, expected to make it with Jesus,
never really make it at all,
don't know how,
some can't
feed themselves,
fool with, *well*—Even some sappy saint said they
look young because pure.[14]

Miller's interest in presenting the experience of the disabled goes beyond her own work. She has recently edited an anthology titled *Despite This Flesh: The Disabled in Stories and Poems*, published by the University of Texas Press.[15] She dedicates her anthology to "Meeme, a child with cerebral palsy supported through the Christian Children's Fund." In her introduction, Miller has this to say:

> The handicapped . . . too often have been and are being killed by kindness, stifled by overprotection, choked by subtle if sometimes unconscious snubs by genuinely good people who would swear to preferring death over hurting anybody. Such treatment, most often misguided rather than intentional, can lead to what Elizabeth Bowen called "the death of the heart." Perhaps the saddest truth, however, is that some of this slow death is self-inflicted; too many handicapped folk linger, bound by anger, depression, self-pity, or fear in the back bedrooms of their own minds. It is to prevent such pointless dying that this anthology has come into being.
>   . . . as editor of *Despite This Flesh*, I have done my best to include in it only material of high literary excellence. Helpful, because if the general public is uninformed it needs to be exposed, and what better means of exposure than good literature?[16]

Larry McMurtry's work is vastly different from that of Vassar Miller, as is his life experience. McMurtry is known for his novels; Miller for her poems. As far as I know, McMurtry has not experienced a serious illness, yet he chose to present one from the patient's point of view in his novel *Terms of Endearment.*[17] Many who have not read the novel *have* seen the film based on the novel. Although the novel and the film are quite different in some ways, both offer interesting narratives of illness from the point of view of the patient and her family. The novel has several themes, but the death of attractive young Emma Greenway Horton from cancer is the climax of the novel as it is of the film. Yet in the 371-page novel, Emma's illness and death occupy only the last nineteen pages.

One morning Emma takes her three-year-old daughter Melanie to the doctor so that both she and Melanie can have flu shots and checkups. After the flu shots, the doctor notices that Emma has two lumps in one of her armpits. This is the beginning of the end for Emma, who turns out to be riddled with melanoma. Very little attention is given to the clinical details of Emma's illness. Rather, the point of view is Emma's: her concern is with what her illness means for her relationships with her family and friends. From the day the doctor gives her the verdict on the biopsy, "'Old girl, you have a malignancy'" (p. 356), everything changes:

> From that day, that moment almost, she felt her life pass from her own hands and the erring but personal hands of those who loved her into the hands of strangers—and not even doctors, really, but technicians: nurses, attendants, laboratories, chemicals, machines. (p. 356)

One of the most significant incidents is the failure of communication between Emma and her doctor about her pain:

> She had never been in pain before and hadn't realized how completely it would come to dominate her. One night not long after she started radium she lost her pills, knocked them off her bed table in the darkness, and found that her bell was out of order. She couldn't get a nurse—all she could do was lie still. Combined with the terrible ache inside her was a sudden deep conviction of helplessness; no one was going to come and help her. For the first time in her life she felt beyond the efficacy of love; all the loved ones she had couldn't help her as much as the little pills lying somewhere in the darkness under her bed.
> Flat on her back, Emma began to cry. When the night nurse looked in on her an hour later there were puddles on

the pillow, on both sides of her head.

The next morning, the memory of it still in her eyes, she asked Dr. Fleming to allow her extra pills in case she spilled some again.

"I can't cope with that much pain," she said honestly.

Dr. Fleming was studying her chart. He looked up and took her wrist efficiently. "Mrs. Horton, pain is nothing," he said. "It's just an indicator."

Emma could not believe she had heard him right. "What did you say?" she asked.

Dr. Fleming repeated it. Emma turned away. She told her mother, who made life harder for Dr. Fleming whenever she could; but Emma knew that even her mother didn't really know what she was talking about. She had never been painfully ill in her life.

By the time she had dealt with pain for a month she had already lost what everyone healthy would have called life—i.e., health. The night of helplessness had turned her away from more than Dr. Fleming. From then on her energies went into an effort to balance herself somehow between drugs, pain, and weakness. (pp. 358-359)

What is primarily conveyed here is the unbridgeable gap between those who suffer intractable pain and those who don't. The gap is understandable in the sense that other people have never experienced what the patient is experiencing. But it is also inexcusable that the physician depicted here makes no attempt to understand what his patient is trying to tell him. He hears her, but he does not listen.

This incident is translated in the film into a much more dramatic episode. Shirley MacLaine, playing Aurora Greenway, comes out of her daughter's hospital room and asks a nurse to give Emma her pain medication. The nurse is busy and brushes Aurora aside. Aurora appeals to another nurse who says that Emma isn't her patient. Ultimately Aurora must throw a fit at the nursing station to get someone to give Emma her pain medication—even though it is past time for Emma's next dose. Aurora screams that her daughter has made it through the prescribed hours between doses, that that is all that her daughter has to do, and that her daughter wants her pain medication NOW. She finally gets it.

Unfortunately, that scene is not as unrealistic as some viewers might think it is. We have perversely insisted in this country that terminally ill cancer patients must not be allowed to medicate themselves. Our fears of drug addiction extend even to the dying, and out of our concern that the dying may become addicted to pain-relieving drugs, historically we have insisted that they wait certain lengths of time between getting pain medication, no matter how bad they hurt in between times. The British are far ahead of us in this regard. One of the most important things that has been learned from the British hospice experience is that if dying patients are allowed to control their own pain medication so that they don't have to fear that their pain will become intolerable before they can get relief, they suffer less and their dying becomes much less difficult for them and for everyone else. What many dying patients fear most is exactly the kind of pain that Emma describes: pain so overwhelming that it dominates everything else and removes patients from the land of the living even before they are dead.

Another thing that reverberates in the experience of many people seeing the film is that even when patients are restricted to receiving pain medication only several hours apart, nurses or other health care professionals can be a little lax about getting the pain medication to the patient as quickly as possible. From their point of view, suffering patients are routine. From the patient's point of view, the need is urgent. The helplessness of Emma, the patient, is perhaps better portrayed in the novel. But that scene in the film better presents the helplessness of the patient's family, in the person of Aurora Greenway, to do anything other than make the patient comfortable. In caring for the patient, family and friends often end up at odds with the health care team. A scene like this from a movie as popular as *Terms of Endearment* can have an important impact—even on members of the medical establishment. One test of worth of a literary work is that it ring true enough to our own life experiences that we can believe it and be moved by it. *Terms of Endearment* does so, and in the filmed version, it does so most effectively in the scene where Aurora Greenway must throw a fit to get medication to relieve her daughter's unremitting pain.

Miller's poems, McMurtry's novel, and many other literary works that present illness from the patient's point of view have much to teach us about human pain and suffering, about empathy, and about medical ethics. We should listen to such stories to learn how we might best respond to patients' needs.

Notes

1. Mel Gussow, "The Time of the Wounded Hero," *New York Times*, 15 April 1979, sec. 2, pp. 1, 30.

2. David Burrell and Stanley Hauerwas, "From System to Story: An Alternative Pattern for Rationality in Ethics," in *Knowledge, Value and Belief*, Vol. 2 of *The Foundations of Ethics and Its Relationship to Science*, ed. H. Tristram Engelhardt, Jr., and Daniel Callahan (Hastings-on-Hudson, N.Y.: The Hastings Center Institute of Society, Ethics and the Life Sciences, 1977), 111-152. All quotations are from this edition and will be cited parenthetically in the text.

3. Larry R. Churchill, "The Human Experience of Dying: The Moral Primacy of Stories Over Stages," *Soundings* 62 (Spring 1979): 24-37. All quotations are from this edition and will be cited parenthetically in the text.

4. Robert Coles, "Medical Ethics and Living a Life," *New England Journal of Medicine* 301 (23 August 1979): 444-446. All quotations are from this edition and will be cited parenthetically in the text.

5. Warren T. Reich, "Experiential Ethics as a Foundation for Dialogue between Health Communication and Health-Care Ethics," presented at the International Communication Association Conference, Honolulu, Hawaii, May 26, 1985. All quotations are from his typescript and will be cited parenthetically in the text

6. See Walter R. Fisher's argument in "Narration as a Human Communication Paradigm: The Case of Public Moral Argument," *Communication Monographs* 51 (March 1984): 1-22.

7. Vicki S. Freimuth, "The 'Story' of the Value Dimension of Health Communication," presented at the International Communication Association Conference, Honolulu, Hawaii, May 26, 1985 (typescript).

8. Obviously, I am talking here about case histories of (ostensibly) physical illnesses rather than case histories of psychoanalytic treatment.

9. For a fuller description and discussion of this experiment, see Rita Charon, "To Render the Lives of Patients," *Literature and Medicine* 5 (1986): 58-74.

10. Reich, 16.

11. Ursula K. Le Guin, *The Left Hand of Darkness* (New York: Ace Books, 1969), 1.

12. Vassar Miller, "Introduction to a Poetry Reading," in *If I Could Sleep Deeply Enough* (New York: Liveright, 1968), ix. Reprinted by permission of Vassar Miller.

13. Vassar Miller, "On the Examination Table," in *If I Could Sleep Deeply Enough*, 38. Reprinted by permission of Vassar Miller.

14. Vassar Miller, "Spastics," in *If I Could Sleep Deeply Enough*, 39. Reprinted by permission of Vassar Miller.

15. Vassar Miller, ed., *Despite This Flesh: The Disabled in Stories and Poems* (Austin: University of Texas Press, 1985).

16. Vassar Miller, "Introduction" to *Despite This Flesh*, xiii-xiv.

17. Larry McMurtry, *Terms of Endearment* (New York: New American Library/Signet, 1975). All quotations from the novel are from this edition and will be cited parenthetically in the text.

Life History, Oral History, and Case History: The Story of Eldrewey Stearns, Integration Leader

Thomas R. Cole

This is the story of the rise, fall, and recovering of an extraordinary man. U.S. Congressman Mickey Leland remembers him as the first major figure of Houston's integration movement. State Senator Craig Washington remembers taking the bus from Prairie View to Houston to walk the picket line under his inspired leadership. Dr. Edith I. Jones, the first black to graduate from medical school at the University of Arkansas, remembers him as the man who led the integration struggle in the streets of Houston.

Ron Stone remembers, too. One day in late 1961 or early 1962, Eldrewey Stearns came to Channel 11's television station for an interview with news director Dan Rather. Stone, then a young reporter for the CBS affiliate, opened the door and invited Stearns in.

"Where's Dan Rather?" Stearns asked aggressively.

"In the next room, putting on his make-up."

"If he gets make-up, I do, too," Stearns demanded.

Flustered, Stone knocked and asked Rather what to do. Dan Rather opened the door and quietly showed him where the make-up was. Stearns took a handful, smeared it on his face, and looked in the mirror at the large white streak across his cheek. The three men stood silently for a moment until Stearns said, "I think I'll just do mine natural." They all burst out laughing and went into the studio for a relaxed and successful interview.

Stone, now news director at Channel 2 TV in Houston, remembers Eldrewey Stearns as an intense and passionate fighter, a "real firebrand." "The one thing you knew about Stearns," he says, "is that he was smart as hell. His mind was always working, and he always had a good grip on the political situation. If he ever could have channeled all that energy and intelligence in one direction, there's no telling what he could have done. But as the years went by, he lost credibility. Much that he did began to seem like a fantasy."

Twenty-five years later, when we regularly mark civil rights anniversaries, celebrate Martin Luther King, Jr.'s birthday, listen to interviews and read autobiographies and scholarly studies of civil rights leaders, his name is conspicuously absent. What ever happened to Eldrewey Stearns? That is for him to tell. But in this era of declining minority enrollment in postsecondary and professional education, and of increasing black poverty, un-employment, and disease, it is particularly fitting that we learn something about the life of a man whose soul is not rested.[1]

I first ran across him in an accident that now seems fated. I did not know that he had been trying to write his life history for almost twenty years, that this was probably his last chance.

We met in a weekly case conference at the University of Texas Medical Branch in Galveston, designed to introduce medical students to the charac-teristics of major mental disorders. As a humanities professor on campus, I brought ethical, cultural, and historical perspectives to bear on the discus-sions that followed interviews with hospitalized patients.

This week's specialty was manic depressive illness, or bipolar affective disorder; the patient was a fifty-two-year-old black man who complained that although he felt very important, no one understood him.

"I've been out of it for three and a half years," he told the psychiatrist. "I haven't been happy since April 25, 1960. I'm always depressed until a new woman or a new bottle comes into the picture." Stearns had been commit-ted to the psychiatric hospital against his will and now felt confused; it was "mysterious," he said. "Everybody was being too nice." At first glance, he appeared to be a disheveled, vulnerable, and angry man whose life had disintegrated under the stresses of poverty, racism, alcoholism, and mental illness; yet his diction was often learned and elegant. Stearns claimed to have drunk enough liquor for twenty-five lifetimes, often blacking out and finding himself in jail. Though doctors had put him on heavy doses of lithium, he chose to "go off it in favor of booze." Previously an inmate at St. Elizabeth's in Washington, D.C., Austin State Hospital, and Jennie Sealy in Galveston, he had been brought to the hospital this time by the mental health deputies, who picked him up from the beach in a drunken state.

A psychiatry resident later recalled seeing him twice in crisis clinic prior to this admission. The first time he had been referred from the emergency room (he had come in complaining of abdominal pain) for his bizarre behavior. Another time he had apparently tried to circumcise himself with a razor, and was eventually referred to a surgeon. He later claimed how proud he was of this—a remark that brought only ridicule from those who might have inquired about the significance of circumcision for a Black man whose great-great grandfather was a German Jewish immigrant.

Surprisingly, this histrionic, vulnerable, angry man spoke in eloquent phrases, though these did not always flow logically from one to another. He claimed to have graduated from Michigan State University, to have received a law degree from Texas Southern University, and to have been the "original integration leader in Texas"—claims that brought doubtful glances from around the room.

Stearns claimed that he had already experienced everything one could desire in life. Marooned on Galveston Island, sleeping on a couch in his parents' living room, he had only one remaining wish: to write his life story and show the world how he "embodied the totality of man's experiences."

As soon as the patient left the room, the psychiatrist turned to diagnostic issues. "What are the positive findings on the mental status exam?" he asked. With no apparent concern for this suffering man, the discussion revolved around criteria for alcoholism and bipolar affective disorder.

"What should we make of the patient's desire to write his autobiography?" I asked.

"A typical expression of grandiosity, a symptom to be included in our diagnostic assessment," was the reply.

"I wonder," I said hesitantly, "if the desire to write one's life story might be a means of cure as well as a symptom." Silence. How could I be so naive as to think that storytelling might be a means of healing this man's broken brain? Why did I think I could develop a relationship of trust with him? Even more, the silence seemed to say, why would anyone want to hear about the life of a poor, crazy black man? It was a gamble, more of one than I ever imagined, but I thought I could find good answers to these questions.

My own academic interests in aging and autobiography had recently sensitized me to the special potential of life stories for both history and psychological growth. According to one school of developmental theory, personal narratives bring the chaotic, disparate events of a life together in a work of productive imagination that transforms that life into a coherent unity.[2]

By imposing a kind of retrospective order on the unpredictable events of a life, personal narratives assist in the achievement of identity. Life stories also rely heavily on reminiscence, which has been associated with increased feelings of well-being or ego integrity in later life.[3] But to be intelligible, life history has to be more than a purely subjective account of one's own life–it has to be "followable," understandable according to our Western belief that all narratives have a beginning, a middle, and an end related to each other in a meaningful manner. Might the long, disciplined effort to create such a narrative have a positive effect on Stearn's inner sense of cohesion and self-esteem?

But autobiographies do not spring forth solely from individual needs, any more than from literary convention. Autobiography is a deeply rooted cultural activity in the modern Western world[4]—especially in the United States, where it builds on the characteristically American compulsion to explain oneself by telling one's story.[5] In Eldrewey Stearns, I soon learned, this compulsion had become an all-consuming obsession.

Autobiography, as William Dean Howells put it prophetically in 1909, is the "most democratic province in the Republic of letters."[6] From Boston Brahmin to Alabama tenant farmer, from spiritual confession to life of crime, autobiography is a powerful means of democratic expression. In creating and re-creating their personal identities, authors offer an interpretation of their recovered pasts. Private, often painful memories become public property, and readers are invited to reality-test and to participate in such recoveries.

"The process of reinventing a plausible and satisfying history," writes Albert Stone, "is therefore very much a collective enterprise. Writer [sometimes collaborator] and readers tacitly conspire to reenter, revivify, and finally understand a singular past which has been consciously remembered and less consciously revised or 'forgotten,' faithfully reproduced in certain respects but extensively imagined in others."[7]

Autobiographies, then, are at once individual stories and cultural narratives, providing the humanities and human sciences with rich sources to explore the interplay between the particular and the general. The personal narratives, for example, of Richard Wright,[8] Zora Neal Hurston,[9] Claude Brown,[10] W.E.B. Dubois[11] or Ossie Guffy[12] have created vivid portraits of what it means to be a person of color in white America. Impressive literary studies[13] and bibliographies[14] document the extent and importance of autobiography as a means of personal expression in the black community.

Despite the literary conceit that genuine autobiography is always the product of a single author, the increasing prominence of collaborative autobiography encouraged me. As I walked to the psychiatric hospital, the artistic power and historical significance of collaborative efforts like *The Autobiography of Malcolm X* and *All God's Dangers* ran through my mind. I knocked on the locked door at the end of the second floor hallway. I wished to speak with Stearns, I told the aide who answered the door.

He took me down to the common room, where Stearns was alternately pacing the floor and looking out the window. I introduced myself and said that I had appreciated the chance to learn about him in the medical student case conference. (He believed that he had been invited there to lecture.)

A short man, clothed in a bright yellow shirt and painter's pants, he looked at me with a fierce gleam through eyes that would later betray great pain and loneliness. Brown skin and salt-and-pepper hair stood out sharply against his yellow shirt. Deep triangular lines on either side of his mustache opened to a mouth spitting out rapid-fire sentences, punctuated by awkward silences.

I told him that I was intrigued by his desire to write his life story and offered to be of help. With reluctance and not a little suspicion, he indicated interest, largely (he said) because he was in no position to refuse. Much later, he admitted that he had assumed I was not up to the task—being younger, white, Jewish, and a Yankee.

While he was still in the hospital, we began meeting in my office once a week. It soon became apparent that he literally could not write due to severe tremors; in the first few sessions he was unable to formulate an outline or a focus of his own. Each time he came in, it seemed that we had to test each other's mettle after the niceties of coffee and a pleasant setting wore off. What did I want out of this? Was this another white man coming to rip him off and leave him stranded? He spoke in grandiose expressions, waving his arms and raising his voice in the manner of a wounded man struggling to create an illusion of power.

After he was discharged, his father began driving him to campus for our sessions; I drove him home when we were finished. Those first few weeks left me confused. Had I taken on too much responsibility for this man's life? Where did my role as a facilitator end and my role as a pseudo-psychotherapist begin? Stearns had refused to return to the hospital on an outpatient basis. He took his lithium irregularly, and he refused to believe that any psychiatrist or psychologist could help him. Yet he showed up at my office without fail at the appointed time every week.

Despite expressions of interest, none of the psychiatrists on the campus were willing to see Stearns in my office. They believed that their therapy might somehow be "tainted" by indulging his autobiographical fantasy or compromised outside the strict confines of the consulting room. However, my friend and colleague, Raymond Fuentes, a child psychologist in the psychiatry department, agreed to meet with us in my office each week to assess Stearns's condition and to provide emotional support and expertise. (Much later, when Raymond was admitted to the hospital for medical tests, Stearns remarked, "At least he'll find out what's wrong with him; I have to tell the whole story to find out what's wrong with me.")

Punctually, this man who seemed to have nothing but a suit of clothes and an old blue travel bag, came to my office to work. We began meeting twice a week to tape his recollections, which revealed an extraordinary memory and imagination. As I suspected, he had an incomparable treasure buried within. The question was, could we rummage around in that memory, invoking its terrible demons and painful disappointments, and return to the present with the story and the man intact.

After two months of searching for early memories amidst awkwardness and mutual confusion of purpose, we reached a brief moment of understanding that gave us both hope for the future of our fragile undertaking. Stearns remarked that working on this book was like going to school again. I asked if he thought he would learn about himself.

"That's right," he replied. "It is a soul searching project, and I pray to God it will become an obsession like the sit-ins and the boycotts and all those other things in my previous life."

"But Eldrewey," I interrupted, "Dr. Fuentes and I don't want it to become an obsession—we want it to become a part of your life and not an escape from it. Do you see what I mean?" "Well . . . right now I can't separate the two. As I've said numerous times, I have already had everything God could give man in one lifetime. Reliving my life to write this book is like heating up yesterday's soup. Anything I get out of this book or this life from now on is an unexpected, welcome bonus."

"What about the possibility that the book may actually be an appetizer?"

"To what?"

"To the next course in your life?"

"Well, then I welcome the main course. If I can get that much light into my life, then I can see the end of the tunnel already. . . ."

"I think that's what we all hope for—that the book will help transform you into someone who doesn't run from himself, someone who has a book to show for his past and can live on into the future. I find it a very exciting possibility."

"Well . . . then . . . there's a twinkle in my eye, and my heart skips a beat to see that you and others have hope when I myself have almost abandoned hope. I am almost a recluse. I go nowhere except around the house, a small five-room bungalow where I live among close relatives. I don't even interact with them; if it weren't for the TV, I would have no communication with the outside world. . . . So I look forward to seeing you every Monday almost as the flowers want for rain."

At the end of that session in late December, we went out to lunch to celebrate the holidays and his fifty-third birthday.

Little by little, signs of change emerged. One cold morning in February, Eldrewey called. His father couldn't drive him because the car was not working, and he had no money for cab or bus fare.

"Why don't you walk?" I asked. "Didn't they call you Rabbit for your quick feet when you were a boy?"

That hadn't occurred to him; it seemed so far and it had been so long since he had been out on his own. "Do you think I can make it in an hour and a half?"

He surprised himself by walking those couple of miles in less than an hour. Feeling both elated and desperate for money, Eldrewey began thinking up ways to support himself while working on the book. He approached the prominent Galveston philanthropist Harris Kempner and requested financial support, giving Kempner my office number. Highly educated and deeply sensitive to human needs, Kempner followed up on this request, which many others would have shrugged off. He called and asked what the book was all about, since he could not understand everything that Eldrewey had said. I told him that I thought it a valuable project but could not confidently predict a completed manuscript. I typed up a proposal for six months of funding, which Kempner agreed to provide out of his own pocket.

During the spring of 1985, while we were meeting twice a week and taping his memories of the late 1950s, Eldrewey began to lose the thread of the story. The content of the sessions moved farther and farther from his own life and into grand pronouncements about his sexual prowess. He became increasingly disorganized, resumed his drinking, and began making sexual advances to female colleagues and office staff.

One day when he came in, his speech was slurred, his breath reeked of alcohol. The session produced only incoherent ramblings on tape and frustration in me, as I realized that I could not prevent him from spinning out of control.

Afterwards, I drove him home and told him that I would not work with him if he came in again with liquor on his breath. He denied that he'd been drinking, and insisted that it was none of my business. I replied that alcohol was off-limits at work; the office was a safe place to work—its rules had to be followed. "I am worried about you," I said. "I hope you will stop drinking and keep yourself together."

The next Monday he failed to appear for the first time. Instead, he began calling several women in the office, asking for dates. Frightened and angry, they rightly turned to me to stop him. I began to wonder—why had I gotten myself into this project that sapped my time and energy, that my colleagues viewed as impossible and dangerous? I spoke on the phone with Eldrewey's mother, who had lived through many such episodes and knew what was coming. "Why does this book take so long, Dr. Cole?" she asked. I tried to be both reassuring and realistic—but she saw through me right away. She said she had to give him money to go out and buy a beer—it was the only way she could have any peace around the house. He had stopped taking his lithium a few days ago; she feared that he would become violent.

I then called Eldrewey, saying that I had missed him and hoped he would come for our next appointment. I repeated that the office was a place for work, not women. His calls to the women continued; their anxiety intensified.

The following week I ran into Eldrewey on the street; he was walking aimlessly, without eyeglasses, drinking a beer wrapped in a brown paper bag. He wore a dirty, light blue shirt, half-tucked into mud-splattered pants. He walked up to me smiling and chattering; shook my hand.

The next day I called him again. "I am worried about you. I think you need help," I said. He muttered something about my wife and hung up. I called Dr. Dott, a senior psychiatry resident who was following his case and said I thought he needed to be hospitalized. She said she would wait until Monday, when he was scheduled to call her.

That weekend, the phone rang in the middle of the night. My wife, the psychiatry resident on call, was needed at the emergency room to see a patient. As we both feared, it was Eldrewey, who had been brought in by a friend and his father. He had gone for several days without sleep or lithium. Though floridly psychotic, Eldrewey agreed with my wife that he needed to be admitted to the hospital. Somehow, amidst great inner turmoil and disorganization, he turned to her and said, "This must be very difficult for you." Later, it became clear that he thought I had admitted him into the hospital. (We were both called "Dr. Cole" and Eldrewey rarely chose to call me by my first name.)

During his first weeks in the hospital, he would barely acknowledge me when I visited. He was furious with me for having interfered with his sex life and for advising him not to drink. "If I had a gun, I'd plug you right now," he said. For the first several visits, which lasted five to ten minutes, I simply told him that I was glad to see him, that I hoped he was feeling better.

One day I brought him a bathing suit so that he could go swimming with the other patients. Slowly, he softened and even expressed pleasure at my visits. It was a relief to see the redness disappear from his eyes, to watch his face regain a shape that reflected some inner reorganization. I mentioned looking forward to resuming work on the book. He looked at me with fear and amazement—as he realized that he hadn't scared me away, that the task of telling his life story remained a real possibility.

Eldrewey continued to improve during the next two weeks while I was away. From New York I sent him a postcard of the Statue of Liberty, then under repair. On that vacation, I ran across a passage from the Gnostic Gospels that articulated my hope for our project:

> If you bring forth what is within you, what is within you
> will save you. If you do not bring forth what is within you,
> what is within you will destroy you.

Before leaving town, I reluctantly agreed with our Institute director that Stearns's presence in the office was causing too much disruption and should not continue. During my absence, the office was moving to a new location in the magnificently restored Ashbel Smith building (better known as "Old Red"). Eldrewey knew this and was looking forward to working there. Rather than risk upsetting him then by telling him that we could not work in Old Red, I decided to wait until I returned.

When I got back to town, he had just been released from the hospital, but nobody knew where he was. He had decided to find an apartment somewhere. On the psychiatric ward, I asked where he was living. A medical student who had taken a liking to him said she thought he had found a place at 24th and Avenue H.

I drove to that corner, got out, and began knocking on doors. Nobody had heard of Eldrewey Stearns. After two hours poking around a neighborhood known in Galveston as "the jungle," I found his landlord. "Oh yeah," he said. "He rents an unfurnished room from me for $25 a week. Nice guy. He lies out here on the front lawn sometimes drinking beer and talking to himself."

"Where is he?" I asked.

"He left here about an hour ago. Said he was going to some Old Red building down there at the medical school."

"Oh shit . . . Thanks."

By the time I got back to the office, it was too late. He had knocked on the door of the office suite, saying he was there for an appointment with me. One of my colleagues came to the door. "Eldrewey," he said in a loud voice, "let's step outside here for a minute."

A shouting match ensued in the hallway; Eldrewey insisted that he was there for an appointment with me. My colleague responded that I was out of the office, that others had already told him to stay away, that he caused great alarm and should not come where he wasn't wanted.

"Who are you to tell me what to do?" demanded Eldrewey. In the meantime, another colleague, alarmed by all the commotion, stepped out into the hall and quietly persuaded Eldrewey to leave. When I arrived at the office, I was greeted with contained fury. "He's harmless," I insisted, without convincing anyone. My shouting colleague was still shaken from the intense confrontation. Furious myself and fearing a major setback, I went back out to find him.

After another hour of driving up and down the streets between the medical school and Eldrewey's apartment, I finally found him, walking with that light blue travel bag. Relieved, I pulled over, rolled down the window and motioned to him to get in. I apologized for the rude reception he had gotten, saying how glad I was to see him. He appeared less upset by the incident than I had feared.

I asked him what had happened. He said that when he had heard someone call him by his first name, he thought it was a welcome, rather than a sign of disrespect from a man who had never met him. "I had been looking forward to showing people the new Eldrewey Stearns over there in the new office." I told him that we couldn't work in Old Red due to his behavior before being hospitalized.

"I owe you an apology," he said.

When we resumed our work, it was August 6, 1985—the fortieth anniversary of the atomic bombing of Hiroshima. Stearns picked up the thread of the narrative right where he had left off, on the verge of his intense and remarkable career as an integration leader.

We began meeting three times a week, and the story flowed more easily. By this time, I had given up my own grandiose fantasies about saving him. Stearns had rejected my naive attempts to help him understand his feelings; likewise, my moralizing about work, women, and alcohol. It seemed that my job was simply to help him tell his life story. Was anything else meddling?

For a while, I thought so. But as his mind spun more and more out of control, I came to see things more clearly. What mattered was my ability to be a listening presence, to help guide the narrative. At times our work created a relationship of dialogue, characterized at its best by a mutuality of inner awareness.

"I had to wait awhile until you got stronger," he said to me later. "You couldn't really handle me at first." "Yes," I replied. "But I'm on to you now." The focal point of our triangular relationship was the story. Each of us had obligations to the other and to the narrative; the balance of these different obligations shifted and the boundaries between them sometimes blurred under stress.

For several months, we discussed the question of coauthorship. I said we could save the decision until later, but that if I ended up extensively editing and revising his words, I wanted to receive credit. If not, I would simply write an introduction, epilogue, or interlude. This idea angered him and the issue smoldered. Finally, after a writer from the *Houston Post* came to Galveston to do an article about him and the book, he made up his mind.

"Okay," he said. "I've got it now. First the book, then me, then you."

This clarity of purpose and priorities did not last long. Continuing stress, mutual disappointment, and recrimination hampered our work. Eldrewey insisted that I did not care enough about him, that I was not devoting enough time to the project. Overcommitted, resentful at his lack of gratitude, I sometimes wished I had never met him.

A few clinical colleagues claimed that I had fallen into a situation I did not really understand: I had stimulated the kind of intense transference that takes place between a patient and therapist; I needed to realize that Eldrewey both loved and hated me in deeply disturbed ways, and that my own psychological responses were woven into the relationship. Several therapists argued that Eldrewey did not really want to finish the book, that he wanted me, and that finishing the book would actually be bad for him. If his whole life was organized around writing this impossible book, what would happen when he no longer had the one thing that gave his life meaning?

I acknowledged these complexities, and refused to yield to them. I resisted my own impulse to abandon the project. In the fall of 1985, we began meeting with Dr. Jaron Winston, a senior psychiatry resident. While managing Eldrewey's drug treatment, Winston provided a supportive space to ease the growing pains of our relationship.

We continued to meet three times a week to tape Eldrewey's reminiscences. He poured himself out in hundreds of hours. His feelings ranged from intense pride and inspiration, to guilt and suicidal despair. His memories ranged from leading the picket line against segregated lunch counters to drinking himself into oblivion and waking up with his pocket picked by the unknown woman he had slept with. There were some tapes filled with pronouncements of his greatness and others with incoherent ramblings.

But by the spring of 1986, Eldrewey had achieved a new ability to focus, to remain on a single subject for more than a few moments. When I asked him if he noticed the difference, he said that he was about seventy-five percent himself and that he almost trusted me. Before leaving town to go into private practice, Winston remarked that the clearer the narrative became, the clearer and more focused Eldrewey became. In April we drove to Rice University, where Eldrewey talked to John Boles's history class on southern autobiography. Watching his troubled performance, the students were both intrigued and disturbed.

But each step forward seemed to result in another step backward. The birth of my daughter in the summer of 1986 precipitated another crisis. I told Eldrewey that I would only meet him twice a week during August, in order to be home with my wife and new baby. I had cancelled all other appointments for that month.

From Eldrewey's point of view, I was not spending enough time on the project to begin with. For a while, he contained his anger to the loud grinding of his teeth. Our sessions then focused on an awful period in the early 1970s, when he was living in New York subways, parks, and back alleys. He remembered the loneliness, hunger, and drunkenness, the frantic womanizing, and the increasingly fantastic efforts to regain political prominence: a scheme to organize an International Black Militia to overthrow apartheid and proclaim himself "the playboy messiah."

Most of the time, Eldrewey genuinely believed that these episodes were legitimate steps in the "paths of a raceman." But one day he turned to me and said that he had achieved only one real success in life: the sit-in movement. "And this book is another one," I replied.

Shortly after my daughter was born, I received a call from the vice-chairman of microbiology department; several women in his department claimed that Stearns was harassing them. He wanted me to control Eldrewey, and took the case to the Office of Affirmative Action, which threatened to ban him from the medical school campus.

Again I was torn between my allegiance to Eldrewey and my allegiance to the University. By now, my protests that he was not dangerous were wearing thin. I referred the affirmative action officer to Dr. Mitchell (who had taken over Eldrewey's care from Jaron Winston), and convinced her to let me warn Eldrewey before the University took legal action.

I called and told Eldrewey that his behavior jeopardized the whole project. His unbidden and persistent advances toward younger white women violated their privacy.

"All I need is some money and some pussy," he replied.

"I don't believe that," I said. "They never made you happy before."

This confrontation marked another turning point in our relationship. For weeks he would not look at me when I came to the sessions. He was all business, presenting a dark and withdrawn countenance. The vertical lines between his eyebrows seemed to grow deeper. His glasses tilted to the left and slipped down to the middle of his nose; red eyes flashed with anger and booze.

In the middle of August, he exploded at me during a session with

Mitchell. I was a "witness for the prosecution," he said; not only was I taking the side of white women and a racist university establishment, but I was cutting back my hours.

"It's because you're a Jew and you're rigid," he shouted. "If my parents die before this book is finished, I'll kill you."

My nerves already frayed from sleepless nights of diapers and bottles, I was shaken by this threat. Feelings of parental vulnerability and protectiveness led me to draw my boundaries more clearly than ever: "My family comes first. If you can find someone else to do a better job with your book, be my guest."

The next few months were sobering. A new distance allowed us both to see things more clearly. Something stabilized in Eldrewey, perhaps mirroring a new firmness in me. I saw how much more would have to go into this narrative than could ever come out of it. And I realized that if I didn't put a limit on the taping, it could go on forever.

Eldrewey read transcripts of our early taping sessions and saw that he had changed. I began to think that his disjointed and chaotic life could not (and should not) be transformed into a smoothly coherent narrative; too much reality would be suppressed in the process. The contradictions, the deep splits in his psyche should be allowed to speak in juxtaposition to one another. My early hopes for his recovery were not realized, but neither were they dashed.

After talking it over, we agreed to conclude the taping in December, 1986, when we would celebrate his fifty-fifth birthday and initiate the book's next phase. Whatever material Eldrewey wanted to include would have to be taped by then. Soon afterward, he began to distinguish between the things he needed to tell me and the things that he wanted to publish. He saw that his whole life could not possibly be put between the covers of a book; it could not all be redeemed.

In October I told Eldrewey that beginning in January I would only meet with him once a week, to begin shaping raw material into chapters. I suggested that it was time to put a pen in his hand. Soon afterward, he appeared in a three-piece suit; he had spent the morning writing in Sandy's Room (named in honor of Harris Kempner's son, who died in Vietnam) at the public library.

Despite valiant efforts, Eldrewey began to fall apart again. We argued about a party we had planned to celebrate completion of the taping. He insisted on a large public gathering to promote the book; I held out for a very small dinner with Mitchell and Eldrewey's parents. In December, after I'd been away for two weeks, he lost interest. He had fallen in love with a blond woman who worked in the Ambulatory Care Building, where we met for our sessions.

"I love her more than you," he said, half realizing what he was saying. "If I had a million dollars, I'd marry her tomorrow and live happily ever after."

"You look like you haven't been sleeping," I said. "Why don't you call Dr. Mitchell?" Without a word, he walked out of the room.

The next day, his mother called. "Eldrewey has changed again, Dr. Cole. He walks around the house talking to himself. Get's worse everyday. He's going to crack up again, and at Christmas time." She asked if I knew what was wrong.

"No," I said disingenuously.

"Well, there's no need of whippin' the devil around the stump. He needs a lady friend . . . But there's nothing we can do but put him in the hands of God to make him stronger." I knew he needed to be hospitalized then, but it took another week. After waiting almost an hour one day for a taping session, I went out to look for him. I found him walking around talking to himself, carrying a coke can wrapped in a brown paper bag. It was rainy and cold; seeing Eldrewey's heavy-lidded, bloodshot eyes and greasy, unshaven face did not raise my spirits any.

"Can I talk to you?" I asked.

"Sure."

"I think you need help. Can I take you to the Crisis Clinic?"

"No," he said, walking off. I followed him down the hallway.

"I'm through with you," he said, walking away again. "I'll pay you for the two-and-a-half years."

The phone rang at home that night. "Dr. Cole, this is Officer Singleton. We have Eldrewey Stearns here. He's all mixed up; been wandering around the campus in the cold rain. We called his mother; she says she can't handle him at home and wants him admitted to the hospital. She gave us your number. Can you come down and take care of him?"

"No, I'm not a physician. But I just talked to Dr. Mitchell, his psychiatrist. Call and he will arrange Eldrewey's admission. If you have any trouble, call me back and we'll find another way." The next time the phone rang, it was Mrs. Stearns. We talked for a long time. She said she hated to see him suffer like this, especially when we had been planning a party to celebrate his accomplishments. She thanked me.

When Steve Mitchell and I visited him in the hospital, he greeted us warmly: "When's the party?" After a moment of silence, he realized it would have to be called off. Then he turned to me—"You're the reason I'm

29

here. It's because you're abandoning the project." I assured him that we were only entering a new phase, in which I'd be less available and he'd carry more of the weight. On the way out of the building, Steve told me that during this psychotic break, Eldrewey thought I was a spy sent to destroy his book.

Actually, he had terminated the taping in his own way. And in the first four months of 1987, he drafted chapters in his own way. He began at the pinnacle: law school days at Texas Southern University; police beatings protested before the Houston City Council; the integration movement at lunch counters, supermarkets, the bus and railway stations; arrests for picketing and for unlawful assembly at Union Station—where the coffee shop owner called the police, he said, because "I don't serve Negroes in my dining room."

When Eldrewey finally put pen to paper, we had reached the point from which I had assumed we would start. If he was not producing great literature, the process of writing was itself a great accomplishment. A new feeling came over me—a kind of detached love, and a commitment not so much to any ultimate product as to the process of self-recreation that emerged from the disciplined narration. Still, I was not surprised when that process broke down again after Eldrewey had written several hundred manuscript pages. His handwriting was illegible; we were forced to return to the slow, expensive process of taping and transcribing. This time he was reading his own drafts, but a large gap emerged between how much he was writing and how much we could tape. Despite continual pressure, I refused to meet more than once a week.

In late April, Eldrewey announced that he would finish the book on July 7 and begin a boycott of Arab, Chinese, and Vietnamese merchants in Galveston. He came to our next session smelling of alcohol; his eyelids had a yellow fluttering, sleepless quality; speech was slurred, thoughts trailed off into himself. I said I thought he needed a break from our work and suggested he call Dr. Mitchell. By June we were back at it. Again we appealed to Harris Kempner for support. Again he agreed to support Eldrewey out of his own pocket and urge the Kempner Fund to pay for tape transcriptions. By summer's end we had agreed to conclude the autobiography with the events of 1960, leaving the subsequent years for a future volume. The impossible book began to seem possible.

When Harris Kempner died in September, we were both shaken. Not only had Harris been a financial benefactor, but his moral support had given us both badly needed confidence. Within days of his memorial service, Mrs. Kempner called. She had been going through Harris's book of charitable contributions and remembered that this project had been important to him. "I don't know this man Stearns," she said, "but I understand that these payments help him keep body and soul together."

"Yes."

"Well, I intend to keep the checks coming.... But I can't understand why Harris had written down that they were to be given for only eight months."

"Because that's what I asked for," I said.

"You dope!" she answered. "Why didn't you ask for a full year? Besides, it's awkward from a bookkeeping standpoint." I was impressed at Ruth Kempner's generosity and her efficiency in carrying out her husband's wishes. I called Eldrewey and gave him this news. He was relieved and bolstered.

The story of Eldrewey Stearns now has a beginning and a middle. As of October 1987, we have recovered his past and saved it from oblivion. And Eldrewey has personally recovered as well from the worst of his sufferings. The conclusion has yet to be written. When finally completed, the life of Eldrewey Stearns will be many things: a confession, a testimony of mental illness and alcoholism, an account of the exploits of a crusading playboy, a memoir of the integration movement and of the problems Blacks face in achieving a stable identity in white America. But its uniqueness will rest on the narrative re-creation of the "totally imperfect" life (as he puts it) that Stearns alone has lived.

Notes

1. Howell Raines, *My Soul Is Rested: Movement Days in the Deep South Remembered* (New York: G. P. Putnam's Sons, 1977).
2. Bertram Cohler, "Personal Narrative and Life Course," in *Life-Span Development and Behavior*, vol. 4, ed. Baltes and Brim (New York: Academic Press); Mark Freeman, "History, Narrative, and Life-span Developmental Knowledge," *Human Development* 27 (1984): 1-9.
3. Robert Butler, "The Life-Review: An Interpretation of Reminiscence in the Aged," *Psychiatry* 26 (1963): 65-76; Marc Kaminsky, *The Uses of Reminiscence: New Ways of Working With Older Adults* (New York: Haworth, 1984).
4. Karl Joachim Weintraub, *The Value of the Individual: Self and Circumstance in Autobiography* (Chicago: University of Chicago, 1978).

5. Alfred Kazin, "The Self as History: Reflections on Autobiography," in *Telling Lives: The Biographers Art*, ed. M. Pachter (Washington, D.C.: Republic, 1979).

6. William Dean Howells, "Autobiography, A New Form of Literature," *Harper's Monthly* 119 (October 1909).

7. Albert E. Stone, *Autobiographical Occasions and Original Acts: Versions of American Identity from Henry Adams to Nate Shaw* (Philadelphia: University of Pennsylvania Press, 1982), 4.

8. Richard Wright, *Black Boy* (New York: Harper and Row, 1945).

9. Zora Neale Hurston, *Dust Tracks on a Road* (Philadelphia: Lippincott, 1942).

10. Claude Brown, *Manchild in the Promised Land* (New York: Macmillan, 1965).

11. W. E. B. DuBois, *The Autobiography of W. E. B. DuBois: A Soliloquy on Viewing My Life from the Last Decade of Its First Century* (New York: International Publishers, 1978). Follows previous volumes published in 1920 and 1940.

12. Ossie Guffy, *The Autobiography of a Black Woman*, as told by Caryl Ledner (New York: Bantam Books, 1971).

13. Rebecca C. Barton, *Witnesses for Freedom: Negro Americans in Autobiography* (Oakdale, N.Y.: Dowling College Press, 1976); Sidonie Smith, *Where I Bound: Patterns of Slavery and Freedom in Black American Autobiography* (Westport, Conn: Greenwood, 1974); Stephen Butterfield, *Black Autobiography in America* (Amherst: University of Massachusetts Press, 1974); John Blassingame, "Black Autobiographies as History and Literature," *Black Scholar* 5 (December 1973/January 1974): 2-9; Roger Rosenblatt, "Black Autobiography: Life as the Death Weapon," *Yale Review* 65 (Summer 1976): 515-27; Michael G. Cooke, "Modern Black Autobiography in the Tradition," in *Romanticism, Vistas, Instances, Continuities*, ed. D. Thornburn and Geoffrey Hartman (Ithaca, N.Y.: Cornell University Press, 1973), 255-80; Elisabeth Schultz, "To Be Black and Blue: The Blues Genre in Black American Autobiography," *Kansas Quarterly* 7 (Summer 1975): 81-96.

14. Russell C. Brignano, *Black Americans in Autobiography: An Annotated Bibliography of Autobiographies and Autobiographical Books Written Since the Civil War* (Durham: Duke University Press, 1974).

"Babe" Didrikson Zaharias:
Her Personal and Public Battle With Cancer

Susan E. Cayleff

> All my life I've been competing—and competing to
> win. I came to realize that in its way, this cancer was the
> toughest competition I'd faced yet. I made up my mind
> that I was going to lick it all the way. I not only wasn't
> going to let it put me on the shelf. I was determined to come
> back and win golf championships just the same as before.[1]

This passage from "Babe" Didrikson Zaharias's 1955 autobiography,
This Life I've Led, reveals the determination and unswerving competitive
nature of the woman the Associated Press named the "Greatest Female
Athlete of the Half Century" in 1950 as she struggled with recurring cancer.

Mildred Ella Didrikson, the multi-talented "Texas Tomboy," was inter-
nationally renowned for her athletic talents. Her victories and near-
legendary feats include: taking two gold medals and a silver at the 1932 Los
Angeles Olympics; scoring over 100 points in a basketball game; driving a
golf ball 327 yards; and winning eighty-two golf tournaments between 1935
and 1953, while becoming the Ladies' Professional Golf Association's
(LPGA) leading money winner for four consecutive years1948-1951.[2]

Exceptional not only for the records she set and a short stint as a
harmonica-playing stage entertainer, Didrikson captured the American
imagination with her Texas-sized bragging, predictions of her successes,
quick quips to the press, and down-home frankness.

Didrikson was to use all of her courage to confront and manage the most
stressful and monumental challenge of her life: her recurring bouts with
cancer. Other than a hernia operation in l952, she had rarely been ill. But
her good health was not to last. As one of her biographers noted:

> The early warnings had been clear enough. A couple of
> months before the diagnosis, she had passed blood. She
> mentioned this to Betty Dodd, [a promising young golfer
> who was an intimate friend of Babe's. Dodd played an
> increasingly vital role throughout Didrikson's illness] who
> told her she must see a doctor and added with terrible
> prescience that this might be a sign of cancer.[3]

Significantly, Betty was the only one to whom Babe confided her own growing fear of cancer. As Babe recalled in her memoirs, "I'd never even hinted at such a thing to George [Zaharias, her husband] . . . I continued to keep my cancer fears a secret from him."[4]

After consulting Dr. Tatum of Beaumont, Babe called Dodd, weeping, and said, "I've got to be operated on. I've got to have a col . . . col . . . ." Dodd recalls that Babe "couldn't say the word. I said, 'Colostomy?' and she said that's right." As Dodd recalls,

> It took ten days to build her up for the operation. I moved into the hospital room with her. George was around, but he kept insisting that she *didn't* have cancer.[5]

The colostomy involved removing the malignancy from the rectum, suturing the anus closed, and re-routing the intestinal tract so that her solid waste passed through an incision in the left side of her stomach. For an athlete whose physical prowess had been her most valued and honed attribute, the psychological anguish of such a procedure was especially acute. Given her earlier charity work on behalf of the Damon Runyan Cancer Fund,[6] Didrikson mused over the irony of her condition and voiced the often-heard lament, "Why me?" Babe recalled her reactions to the diagnosis:

> We didn't talk much. Big George, three hundred pounds of man, had tears in his eyes, and he wasn't ashamed of them, either. And I, well, I guess I was numb. The real terror was to come later. Right then all I could seem to think of was—Why did it have to happen to me?[7]

The operation was performed at the Hotel Dieu in Beaumont on April 17, 1953; Dr. Robert Moore of the University of Texas Medical Branch at Galveston was the surgeon and Tatum assisted.[8] After more than four hours of surgery, Dr. Moore conferred with Betty Dodd and George Zaharias and told them that more cancer had been found in Babe's lymph nodes. As Betty recalls:

> The colostomy had gone well, but he felt that within another year she would have more trouble. He said he thought it might be wise not to mention this bleak news to Babe . . . . George was crying, I don't think he heard a word Moore said. I just put the whole thing out of my mind.[9]

It appears that Betty and George, the two people closest to Babe, followed Moore's advice and concealed from Babe that some cancer still remained despite the surgery. This concealment may have accounted in large
part for the series of events that followed. Even prior to her colostomy,
Didrikson had requested, through the AP wire service, "that instead of
flowers, please send all contributions to the cancer fund."[10] Just two hours
before surgery, Bill Scurlock, a sports editor who was a personal friend of
Babe's, was summoned to her bedside where he found her "cheerful,
courageous and smiling with her usual quips." Babe remarked to Scurlock,
"I'm tired of being on the sports page. Put me on page one."[11]

Put on page one she was. Believing her cancer cured, Babe scoffed at
Tatum's suggestion that she might never be able to play golf again. Simul-
taneously with her post-operative strengthening, the press helped bolster,
if not create, the David vs. Goliath metaphor that so informed her three-year
struggle with the disease.

Using sports imagery, Babe's cancer became, alternately, the "hole she
couldn't birdie," the "hurdle she could leap," the "roughest contest of her
life," the "course she must run," and in her own words, using golf as a
metaphor, the "biggest competitive round of my life." "I'm not out of the
rough yet!," she commented.

Babe herself set the tone for the press coverage of her ailment. For
example, she compared her 1953 cancer diagnosis to the unsettling ruling
in 1935 that since she had turned pro she could not participate as an
amateur. Babe recalled in 1955:

> I didn't do any sounding off myself. When you get a big
> setback like that, there's no use crying about it. It was
> something like the time in 1953 when I found out I had
> cancer. You just have to face your problem and figure out
> what to do next.[12]

Following her lead, four months after the colostomy, a 1953 *Time* article,
"The Babe is Back," featured a photograph of Babe swinging a golf club with
the caption, "Golfer Zaharias: The muscle is spiritual."[13] The article went
on to say that Babe took the news of her cancer

> . . . as calmly as she takes one of her rare setbacks on a
> golf course. "I'll beat it," she said . . . . Last week, with
> doctors marveling at her recuperative power (the Babe
> calls it "spiritual muscle") she was back on the golf course
> playing in Chicago's Tam O'Shanter tournament.[14]

But it would trivialize Babe's psychic and athletic comeback to attribute her re-entry into competitive golf solely to her lack of knowledge of her cancer, or to media hyperbole. Didrikson, because she viewed her recovery as a contest, was able to use the media to further her own ends, much as she had done as a competitor. Further, by relying on the athletic model that stressed endurance, striving for "personal bests," and public approval, Babe knowingly surrounded herself with familiar and successful life-strategies.

A strategy that became increasingly vital for Babe's well-being was her activism on behalf of cancer education and fund raising, an activism that began on her fortieth birthday with the inauguration of Babe Didrikson Zaharias Week, June 22-28, 1953. Nearly two thousand golf courses cooperated in Zaharias Week with all proceeds going to the Damon Runyan Cancer Foundation.[15]

Returning to the links a mere fourteen weeks after her surgery, Babe finished third in the Tam O'Shanter tournament.[16] The next week she finished third in the World Golf Championship.[17] In May, 1954, Babe won five tournaments including the U. S. Women's Open Golf championship.[18] As the press reported her victory, a crowd of six thousand watched her finish twelve strokes ahead of her nearest rival. Following her last putt and a roar from the crowd, Babe was immersed in a flood of hugs and kisses from George, Betty, and rival golfers. Babe phoned her doctors from the course, and when she thanked Dr. Robert Moore for all he'd done, Moore replied, "You did it yourself, Babe . . . . It was your faith, Babe . . . that and your courage."[19]

Babe had developed close and meaningful relationships with her physicians and their families, so that sharing her victory with them was a natural extension of the bond between them. Peter Moore, a present-day Galvestonian and son of Dr. Moore, Babe's personal physician, remembers social and informal visits to his house by Babe, George, and Betty. Peter remembers Babe as warm, cheerful, and stoic; essentially no talk centered around her cancer, attributable perhaps to both her sense of "being cured" and the youthful ears of the listener, Peter, a teenager struck with the magnitude of the celebrity in his home.[20] Similarly, Babe and George socialized frequently with Drs. Martin and Rose Schneider. The former, now deceased, was the head of Radiotherapy at the University of Texas Medical Branch (UTMB) at the time. Rose Schneider today remembers Babe as a charming, warm, and stoic woman.[21]

Despite her 1954 athletic accomplishments, physical developments did not bode well for Didrikson. On a fishing trip in the spring of 1955, Babe, determined to dislodge her vehicle, which had become stuck in the sand, shovelled vigorously. She was awakened that night by a terrible back pain, attributed it to the shovelling, and sought immediate help through painkillers. Retrospectively, Betty surmised, "Now that I look back, this was the beginning of the end. The cancer had returned but it took months to find it."[22]

Babe's tumor record from John Sealy Hospital at UTMB, where she moved after tests in Beaumont brought neither answers nor relief, reveals little about the cause of her pain. A June 17, 1955, medical chart entry states:

> Pt was doing well until October 1954 when severe pain in rt. buttock, leg and calf began following an apparent injury described as trying to move an automobile which was stuck, and after stamping a golf ball into the ground with her rt foot. Pain has been intermittent since then becoming more severe and more continuous.[23]

On June 22, 1955, Babe was operated on by Dr. Snodgrass at John Sealy for the removal of a herniated disk in her back,[24] then thought to be the cause of her pain.

On August 5, Babe was told she had "a small cancer lesion" in the pelvic area.[25] Warning signs of this, vaginal bleeding that had occurred for at least three months prior to the second diagnosis of cancer, had not been noted in her medical chart until August 4.[26] It is unknown whether Babe concealed this bleeding, thinking it irrelevant. On the day the cancerous lesion was found, an innovative x-ray treatment, designed to alleviate her recurring pain, commenced.[27]

George Zaharias, skilled at manipulating reporters from his professional wrestling days as "The Crying Greek from Cripple Creek," met the press on this day and told them the Babe ". . . took the bad news like the mighty champion she had always been . . . she's not giving up . . . She never flinched when told she had another cancer."[28] In an eery twist of literary premonition, Babe's autobiography ends on August 5, the day the x-ray treatments began.

Babe's enduring optimism in the face of the physical pain she endured can be explained in part by her desire to keep the LPGA going strong. More important, her attitude reflected her commitment to serve as a role model for other cancer patients. In response to the oft-asked question, why didn't she just quit pro golf, fade from public life, and take it easy in 1955, she responded:

> There are several reasons why I didn't retire from golf after that 1953 cancer business—and still don't intend to retire, —

in spite of my 1955 ailments. One reason is that every time
I get out and play well in a golf tournament, it seems to
buck up people with the same cancer trouble I had.[29]

Only fifteen or sixteen days after her colostomy, Babe held a press
conference from her hospital bed. Recalling how she set her hair in
preparation for the cameras, she said,

"I knew that it would encourage other cancer patients if
they saw me get well. I wanted the public to know I was
alright."[30]

Another example of Babe's influence occurred when another patient in
the Hotel Dieu refused a colostomy. At Babe's urging, the patient relented
and permitted the surgery to be performed.[31] In short, Babe had a profound
impact on other cancer patients as one who "went public" with the disease
—in an era when this was rarely done.

Her influence on cancer education and fund raising was similarly
immense: from her hospital bed in John Sealy Hospital in Galveston, on
September 12, 1955, Babe and George announced The Babe Didrikson
Zaharias Fund, Inc.[32] As one news release characterized the scene, "A bit
weak from her long hospital stay . . . Babe was smiling big as she announced
the establishment of the . . . fund from a sun porch at the hospital."[33] As Babe
stated, the purpose of the Fund was "to help the needy people who are not
able to pay to find out if they have cancer."[34]

"Those who were not financially able to undergo long periods of
examination and observation"[35] were a special concern to Babe. In fact, Dr.
Rose Schneider of UTMB, whose husband served on the original Babe
Didrikson Zaharias Cancer Fund Board of Directors, remembers Babe's
sense of gratitude to UTMB, where Babe's father, Ole Didrikson, who also
died of cancer, was treated.[36] This gratitude to UTMB (whose teaching
hospital treats people regardless of ability to pay) largely accounts for
Babe's decision to receive her own treatment at the University, as well as to
establish her Cancer Fund there.

The nonprofit Fund's first project was the establishment of a tumor clinic
at UTMB. Beyond that, "funds were to be used to assist established tumor
clinics and cancer treatment centers in employing well-trained technicians
and financing most of the advanced equipment."[37] At the Fund's opening
day ceremonies John W. McCullough, one of the board's directors, contributed the first $1,000, which George matched on behalf of Babe and himself.[38]

Two days after the Fund commenced on September 14, Babe left the hospital with Betty, who had stayed by her side during her hospitalization, and with George, who was accompanying her to their home in Tampa, Florida. A notation on her medical chart the day she left the hospital says:

> From a psychologic viewpoint, I think it would be prefer-
> able to allow her to ret. to her own (sic) home for a time, with
> sufficient narcotics to remain comfortable. When symp-
> toms become worse, chorodotomy or some other proce-
> dure could be performed.[39]

Throughout 1955 and 1956 Babe and George continued their efforts on behalf of the Babe Zaharias Open, an annual Beaumont event since 1953,[40] and the Cancer Fund. A June 4, 1956, letter addressed to sports editors nationwide, printed on the Fund's letterhead, explains that the Fund's board (as well as Governor Allan Shivers of Texas, and the Governor of Florida)[41] "has honored me by designating the month of June Babe Zahar-ias Cancer Fund Month, as my birthday is June 26."[42]

The letter requested that the editors publicize and cover tournaments in their area. Babe concluded the personally signed letter with "I believe the Fund can help a great deal in the fight against cancer, and I will personally appreciate your cooperation in this effort."[43]

Throughout the remainder of 1955 Babe resided in Tampa with George and Betty. Although at times she felt well enough to play golf, on occasion she was unexpectedly overwhelmed with pain. The pain centered in her left foot as "the cancer had affected the sciatic nerve that ran down her leg."[44]

Babe, unable to bear the pain in her leg and foot, returned to John Sealy Hospital in Galveston in December of 1955 and stayed there until the end of January 1956.[45] In March of 1956, Babe asked to return to the Galveston hospital where she remained until her death.[46]

At an LPGA tournament in June of 1956, held in honor of Babe's forty-third birthday, Betty raised approximately $5,000 for the Cancer Fund.[47] Less than a month later, Babe underwent a chorodotomy—"a surgical divi-sion of the nerve tract of the spinal cord"—to relieve her pain.[48]

Hovered over by the press during her bouts with cancer, Babe's personal struggle took on Olympian proportions in the public eye. Article titles alone give ample evidence of the role she had come to play as a symbolic *survivor* of cancer: "The Girl Who Lived Again,"[49] "Cheerful Babe Continues Stub-born Battle Against Cancer as 42nd Birthday Nears,"[50] "Babe Loses Strength, Weight But Continues to Put up Fight,"[51] "Babe's Grit Praised by

Physicians,"[52] "Physicians Report Babe Doing Well,"[53] and "Tributes from World Over Pour Down on Babe at Birthday Party."[54] Illustrated in this coverage of her trials, both Babe and the press used the familiar athletic/ competitive framework to make sense of and cope with her debilitating illness. The press coverage of Babe's decline, cloaked as it was in sports metaphor, was made palatable to an American public all too prone to deny—and back away from—the ugly realities of the disease.

As for Babe, she chose to cloak her struggle in sports metaphor; she was never quite at ease or totally self-revealing in publicly discussing her pain or her dying. In private and in public Babe refrained from emotionalism. Even without employing sentimentality she knew how to mobilize the public. She understood the infatuation of fans for an athlete and she used that infatuation to involve her fans in her cancer fight. The American public became the audience for her struggle through carefully orchestrated press conferences from her bedside. This was done at some personal sacrifice. At times the press coverage seemed invasive and almost circus-like, particularly upon her death. As one biographer remarked of this coverage: "Babe deserved better. Her death was so agonizing, so public, so sensationally reported that it is only now possible to see her in perspective . . ."[55]

Through this mutually caring, yet somewhat exploitive relationship between Babe and the press, cancer became mentionable and tolerable to the American people. Her personality, coupled with the media's packaging of her illness coalesced to make her symbolic, to many, as the one who could lick what one reporter called "The Black Beast" of cancer.[56]

Babe Didrikson Zaharias died at John Sealy Hospital on September 27, 1956, at age 45. Indicative of the portrayals of her death is the following excerpt from the *New York Times*:

> Babe Didrikson Zaharias has finally lost the big one. It was after the greatest and most gallant struggle of her great and gallant career. This one was the hardest to lose, but she knew that "you can't win them all" and that there is one antagonist against which even the stoutest heart is not quite defense enough. . . . She didn't know the meaning of the word quit, and she refused to define it, right to the end.
>
> Her tragic death must spur us to renewed efforts to fight the foe that cut her down. But her own terrific fight against that foe can also be an inspiration to all those who must face and overcome handicaps. It is not only the annals of sport that her life has enriched. It is the whole

story of human beings who somehow have to keep on trying.[57]

Babe's legacy as a sports figure[58] is matched by her legacy as a medical humanitarian; the Zaharias Golf tournaments and the Zaharias Cancer Fund distinguish her as one committed to both women's professional golf and cancer education. Babe realized that her medical treatment would attract national attention. Her stated goal throughout in going public with her ailment was to minimize the fear, uncertainty, and sense of isolation experienced by others in her condition.

Her efforts on behalf of cancer education were successful and greatly appreciated, evidenced by the award she received from the American Cancer Society in 1954.[59] She also received the award of the Public Health Cancer Association of America "for contributing the nation's most outstanding service in cancer education and control."[60] Further, she garnered the esteem and gratitude of the John Sealy Hospital Staff, as symbolized by the plaque in the corridor of the Radiotherapy Department commemorating her efforts that culminated in the purchase of a then top-of-the-line radioactive cobalt machine for UTMB.[61] And, finally, a resolution was passed in the Texas House of Representatives on January 22, 1957, paying tribute to "the memory of this gallant Texas lady . . . for her athletic career" and "her dramatic fight against cancer . . ."[62] Babe's contributions to cancer education and treatment were substantial. And yet her legacy on the cancer issue was created by the press even prior to her death. Her heroism in sport was transformed into an even greater heroism in her premature death. A (circa) 1955 press release announcing the Zaharias Cancer Fund has a tantalizing prophetic ring. Babe, the author notes, gave the world far more than athletic accomplishments: "She has already enriched posterity with the most valuable gift of all—the Babe Didrikson Zaharias Fund for the cancer needy . . . That's Babe's big gift to the world."[63]

In a sense, the glowing portrayal of Babe is warranted. Buffeted by personal anguish and public expectation, Babe gracefully balanced her fear, uncertainty, and public persona. One of the first to go public with her cancer, she served as an inspirational model for others in similar circumstances.[64] Further, her fund-raising activities distinguish her as one whose concern for quality care extended to others less materially fortunate. In this final contest, her true mettle emerged.

During her battle with cancer, Babe evolved from a self-centered athlete to a bonafide humanitarian. For Babe, the athletic and the medical models merged to help her combat the common adversary: cancer. As she had so many times before, she invited the fans, the media, and even the medical team to be a part of her action.

Yet, despite all of Babe's and the press' hyperboles, Babe's legacy to the American public on the cancer issue was mixed. She surely provided a much needed consciousness- and fund-raising role for a nation that experienced with her, her own struggle against cancer. She posed at the same time, however, as one ready, and perhaps even able, to emerge victorious over *any* foe, including cancer. This very bravado that sheltered her adoring public from her uncertainties and distresses was *misleading*. It cloaked the precise sentiments and isolationism that so characterized her own travail and the experiences of other cancer patients. As a result, rather than offering to other cancer patients a realistic model of genuine communicativeness, introspection, and resolution, Babe's bravado offered instead a conqueror's independent stoicism. For other cancer patients and their supportive kin this suggested an unrealistic model that demanded of them denial, courage, good humor, and distorted hope—a tempting and disturbing model for an American public that all too eagerly denies and avoids the frightening and bewildering "black beast of cancer" and its patients.

Notes

1. Babe Didrikson Zaharias (as told to Harry Paxton), *This Life I've Led: My Autobiography* (New York: A. S. Barnes, 1955), 5.
2. Zaharias, "The 'Babe' A Record of Achievement, Mildred (Babe) Didrikson Zaharias 1914-1956" (A leaflet distributed by the Babe Didrikson Zaharias Foundation, Inc., Beaumont, Texas: condensed from W. R. Schroeder and Thad S. Johnson, "WHO in Sports"); William O. Johnson and Nancy Williamson, "Babe, Part 3," *Sports Illustrated* (20 October 1975); Betty Hicks, "Babe Didrikson Zaharias 'Stand back! This ain't no kid hittin,'" *Women's Sports* (November 1975): 24-28; and Bruce Biossat, "Accolade for Babe," *NEA*, editorial (28 September 1956), document #11.1.10.5 the BDZ papers at the John Gray Library, Lamar University, Beaumont, Texas. Babe just missed a third gold on a technicality; her winning golf streak also included seventeen consecutive amateur victories in 1946-47.
3. William Oscar Johnson and Nancy P. Williamson, *"Whatta-Gal" The Babe Didrikson Story* (Boston: Little, Brown and Company, 1975), 205.
4. Zaharias, *This Life I've Led* . . . , 199.
5. Johnson and Williamson, *"Whatta-Gal"* . . . , 206.
6. Zaharias, *This Life I've Led* . . . , 201.

7. Babe Didrikson Zaharias (as told to Booton Herndon), "'I'm Not Out of the Rough—Yet!,'" periodical unidentified, document #11.1.13.23 BDZ papers at JGL.

8. "Babe Zaharias Goes Under Knife at Hotel Dieu Here Today," *Beaumont Journal* (17 April 1953), document #11.1.6.13 BDZ papers JGL; and "Final Hospital Pix," unidentified source (18 May 1953), document #11.1.6.13 BDZ papers JGL.

9. Johnson and Williamson, *"Whatta-Gal"* . . . , 206.

10. "Babe Zaharias Goes Under Knife . . . "

11. Ibid.

12. Zaharias, *This Life I've Led* . . . , 98.

13. "The Babe is Back," *Time* (10 August 1953): p. 1 of 2 unnumbered.

14. Ibid.

15. "Babe Zaharias Goes Under Knife . . . "

16. Babe Biographical by Tiny Scurlock (page 4 only), document #11.1.1.2 BDZ papers JGL; and "Wilson Information, Press, Radio, TV: [Babe Zaharias only]," 1954, document #11.2.20.3 BDZ papers JGL.

17. Johnson and Williamson, *"Whatta-Gal"* . . . , 209-10; and "Wilson Information . . . ", 1953, document #11.2.20.2 BDZ papers JGL. Her performance at the Tam O'Shanter enabled her to edge out Ted Williams of the Boston Red Sox (who had just returned from Marine duty in Korea) as the Ben Hogan Comeback of the Year recipient.

18. Johnson and Williamson, "Babe, Part 3," *Sports Illustrated* (20 October 1975).

19. "Fund for Detection of Cancer Established by Babe Zaharias," *Beaumont Enterprise* (12 September 1955): 11, document #11.1.7.2 BDZ papers JGL.

20. Interview conducted 20 February 1985 with Peter Moore, son of Dr. Robert Moore of Galveston, Texas.

21. Interview conducted 20 February 1985 with Dr. Rose Schneider, wife of Dr. Martin Schneider. The latter was Chief of Radiotherapy at John Sealy Hospital, University of Texas Medical Branch, Galveston, Texas, during Babe's hospitalizations. The Schneiders socialized frequently with the Zahariases.

22. Johnson and Williamson, *"Whatta-Gal"* . . . , 211; and for a full chronology of Babe's illness and hospitalizations, see Babe Biographical by Tiny Scurlock (page 4 only), document #11.1.1.2 BDZ papers JGL.

23. See Tumor Record, History No. #5554-K, Zaharias, Mrs. Mildred, John Sealy Hospital, University of Texas Medical Branch, Galveston, Texas #4721-105.0, Treatment Sheet 6/17/55. BDZ's chart spans 4/22/54

through 6/22/55. A notation in the upper-right front page reads "Exp. 9-27-56."

24. Tumor Record, 5534-K (sic), John Sealy Hospital, Treatment Sheet, 6/22/55.
25. AP release out of Galveston, Texas, "Babe Zaharias Gets Treatment for New Cancer" (5 August 1955), document #11.1.8.1 BDZ papers JGL; and AP release out of Galveston, Texas, "Babe Rests in 2nd Bout With Cancer" (7 August 1955), document #11.1.8.2. BDZ papers JGL.
26. Tumor Record 5554-K John Sealy Hospital, Chart Entry 8/4/55.
27. AP release out of Galveston, Texas, "Babe Zaharias Gets Treatment...";
and AP release out of Galveston, Texas, "Babe Rests in 2nd Bout ... "
28. "Babe Zaharias Gets Treatment For New Cancer" (5 August 1955), document #11.1.8.1. BDZ papers JGL.
29. Zaharias, *This Life I've Led . . .* , 228-29.
30. Ibid., 214.
31. Ibid.
32. Zaharias Cancer Fund Story [Sports Guide], document #11.1.1.18 BDZ papers JGL; The Babe Didrikson Zaharias Fund, information, document #11.1.7.1. BDZ papers JGL; and "Fund for Detection of Cancer Established by Babe Zaharias," *Beaumont Enterprise* (12 September 1955): 11, document #11.1.7.2. BDZ papers JGL.
33. "Fund for Detection of Cancer Established . . . "
34. Ibid.
35. Zaharias Cancer Fund Story, p. 1 of 2, document #11.1.1.18 BDZ papers JGL.
36. Interview 19 February 1985 with Dr. Rose Schneider, University of Texas Medical Branch, Galveston, Texas.
37. Zaharias Cancer Fund Story, p. 1 of 2, document #11.1.1.18 BDZ papers JGL. The Fund's Board of Directors included Dr. Robert Moore, Babe's surgeon; Fred Corcoran of New York, her manager and personal friend; Dr. John Otto, Dr. John Childers, Dr. Hyman W. Paley, and Dr. Martin Schneider, all of the University of Texas Medical Branch at Galveston; V. W. McLeod, Galveston attorney; Judge C. G. Dibrell of Galveston; and John W. McCullough, president of Galveston's Hutchings Sealy National Bank and chairman of the Sealy-Smith Foundation, which gave John Sealy Hospital to the University. Ibid., "Fund for Detection of Cancer Established by Babe Zaharias," *Beaumont Enterprise* (12 September 1955): 11, document #11.1.7.2. BDZ papers JGL.
38. Ibid., ibid.
39. Tumor Record 5554-K, John Sealy Hospital, 9/14/55; her physician at

this time was Dr. Snodgrass.

40. Babe Biographical by Tiny Scurlock, document #11.1.1.2 BDZ papers JGL. The Beaumont Tournament was won by Babe in 1953; she placed second in 1954 and 13th in 1955. Ibid.
41. Zaharias Cancer Fund Story, document #11.1.1.18 BDZ papers JGL.
42. Form letter to sports editors under letterhead "The Babe Didrikson Zaharias Fund, Inc," document #11.1.7.3. BDZ papers JGL.
43. Ibid. The letter, significantly, has a graphic in the lower right-hand corner with the initials BDZ with a superimposed key, signalling perhaps her desire to unlock the mysteries of the disease.
44. Johnson and Williamson, *"Whatta-Gal"* . . . , 213.
45. Ibid., 215-16. Returning to Tampa in February, Babe used her waning strength to travel to Sarasota to watch Dodd on the eighteenth green of a tournament she had a chance to win. Unfortunately, Dodd lost by one stroke.
46. Ibid., 216-17. On this vigil, her sister Lillie moved to Galveston and acted as her help-mate.
47. Ibid., 217.
48. "Pain Relief Operation Done on Babe," unidentified newspaper (13 July 1956), document #11.1.8.5 BDZ papers JGL; and "Babe's Pain Easing After Operation," unidentified newspaper (14 July 1956), document #11.1.8.6 BDZ papers JGL.
49. Quentin Reynolds, "The Girl Who Lived Again," *Reader's Digest* (October 1954): 50-55.
50. "Cheerful Babe Continues Stubborn Battle Against Cancer as 42nd Birthday Nears," unidentified newspaper (26 June 1956), document #11.1.8.3 BDZ papers JGL.
51. "Babe Loses Strength, Weight But Continues to Put Up Fight," unidentified newspaper (25 August 1956), document #11.1.8.8. BDZ papers JGL.
52. "Babe's Grit Praised by Physicians," UP release (29 August 1956), document #11.1.8.11 BDZ papers JGL.
53. "Physicians Report Babe Doing Well," AP release (15 July 1956), document #11.1.8.7 BDZ papers JGL.
54. "Tributes from World Over Pour Down on Babe at Birthday Party," AP release (27 June 1956), document #11.1.8.4 BDZ papers JGL.
55. Johnson and Williamson, "Babe, Part 3," *Sports Illustrated*, p. 7 of 7.
56. Bill Scurlock, "Babe Is Warm Personal Memory," *Beaumont Journal* (28 September 1956), document #11.1.10.1 BDZ papers JGL.
57. "Babe Didrikson Zaharias," *New York Times*, undated document

#11.1.10.2 BDZ papers JGL; also see "Finally She Had to Lose," *Life* (8 October 1956): 169-70, document #11.2.19.1 BDZ papers JGL. The article notes that even the President of the United States was moved to say, "Every one of us feels sad that finally she had to lose."

58. Attested to by her selection as Woman Athlete of the Year by the Associated Press six times (1931, 1945, 1946, 1947, 1950, and 1954), a feat matched by neither man nor woman. Hicks, "Babe Didrikson Zaharias 'Stand Back! . . . '"; and Schroeder and Johnson, "WHO in Sports," as reprinted in "The 'Babe' A Record of Achievement . . . ," distributed by BDZ Foundation, Inc., Beaumont, Texas.

59. The plaque reads as follows: The American Cancer Society Institute, 1954 Certificate of Appreciation to Babe Didrikson Zaharias for Noble Assistance in the Crusade to Conquer Cancer. The American Cancer Society Certificate of Appreciation resides in the Babe Didrikson Zaharias Memorial Museum, Beaumont, Texas.

60. Official copy of House Simple Resolution No. 41, State of Texas House of Representatives, honoring Babe Didrikson Zaharias, 22 January 1957, document #11.1.11.2 BDZ papers JGL.

61. The plaque honoring Babe Didrikson Zaharias still resides in the corridor in the University of Texas Medical Branch Radiotherapy Department. It usually hangs alongside a photograph of Babe (in a polka dot dress) with her physician, Dr. Robert Moore, dated circa 1955. It reads as follows:

> In Memory of
> Mildred Didrikson Zaharias
> Who, With Her Husband, George,
> Contributed Generously in Time And
> Money For The Purchase of Equipment
> In This Room

62. House Simple Resolution No. 41, State of Texas House of Representatives . . . , document #11.1.11.2 BDZ papers JGL.

63. Zaharias Cancer Fund Story, document #11.1.1.18 BDZ papers JGL.

64. Sandra Hansen Konte, "I Will Get Well, If You Let Me," *Cancer News* (Autumn 1984): 2. Konte recalls "the old friend," who, in trying to reassure Sandra that she will recover, "spent an afternoon telling me about Babe Didrickson (sic) Zaharias's cancer surgery—and her agonizing death after a relapse." While Babe's *outcome* may not have been reassuring, her will throughout was, and is still being invoked to bolster cancer patients thirty years posthumously.

Caring for Congenitally Handicapped Newborns

Ronald A. Carson

One month after the highly publicized death of Baby Doe in a Blooming-ton, Indiana hospital on April 15, 1982,[1] the Secretary of the Department of Health and Human Services, at the direction of President Reagan, reminded all hospitals receiving federal funding that Section 504 of the Rehabilitation Act of 1973 makes it "unlawful . . . to withhold from a handicapped infant nutritional sustenance or medical or surgical treatment required to correct a life-threatening condition, if: (1) the withholding is based on the fact that the infant is handicapped; and (2) the handicap does not render the treatment or nutritional sustenance medically contraindicated." The May 1982 reminder received little attention in the professional literature and was scarcely noticed by the press. Nearly a year passed.

Then, on March 7, 1983, a tougher regulation appeared in the *Federal Register* authorizing HHS officials to take "immediate action" to protect endangered infants and requiring hospitals to make their records available to members of "special assignment Baby Doe squad team[s]" upon request. The Baby Doe regulation was to take effect on March 22, two weeks short of the end of the customary thirty-day comment period. In support of the emergency action, Surgeon General C. Everett Koop observed, "Americans have been shocked and appalled at the reported deaths of handicapped infants who have been deliberately allowed to die by denial of treatment."

But District of Columbia Federal District Court Judge Gerhard A. Gesell ordered the "Baby Doe" regulation withdrawn on procedural grounds. Formally titled "Nondiscrimination on the Basis of Handicap," the regula-tion required over 6,000 hospitals nationwide to post a notice in a conspicu-ous place in delivery rooms and newborn nurseries declaring that "Dis-criminatory failure to feed and care for handicapped infants in this facility is prohibited by federal law." The notice also displayed the toll-free number of a "handicapped infant hotline" available twenty-four hours a day to "any person having knowledge that a handicapped infant is being discrim-inatorily denied food or customary care." In a suit brought by the American Academy of Pediatrics and the National Association of Children's Hospi-tals and Related Institutions against HHS, Judge Gesell ruled that ". . . the public interest required that the regulation not continue in effect." Gesell commented further that, in addition to having acted in "haste and inexperience" HHS had provided no definition of "customary medical care" and had apparently disregarded the recommendations of the President's Commission for the Study of Ethical Problems in Medicine and Biomedical and Behavioral Research.

The President's Commission recommended that the best interests of an infant should be pursued when those interests are clear. When they are ambiguous, parental discretion should be allowed. Parents should be assumed to speak for their seriously ill newborn unless there is an unresolvable disagreement between them, or they are disqualified from decision making on grounds of incompetence, or their decision is clearly against the infant's best interest. The medical staff and administration of each institution caring for severely ill newborns should ensure that the institution has clear and explicit policies that require review of decisions to forego life-sustaining treatment and of situations in which physicians and parents disagree as to what is in an infant's best interest.

A revised federal regulation, which went into effect on May 15, 1985, is the result of two years of sometimes heated debate and negotiation involving Congress, the courts, and various public agencies, professional associations, and lay organizations. Its aim is to ensure that no infant becomes a victim of medical neglect.[2] In order to qualify for federal child abuse prevention grants, states must have procedures in place for responding to allegations of medical neglect.

Children's Protective Services in Texas are provided through ten administrative regions that encompass 254 counties housing over 1,000 hospitals. The Office of Children's Protective Services of the Texas Department of Human Services conducts approximately 70,000 child abuse and neglect investigations annually. In the event that the responsible regional staff member receives an allegation that an infant is being denied medically indicated life-saving treatment, the State CPS office is to be notified. The responsible staff member in that office contacts the hospital administrator and chief-of-staff at the hospital in question to inform them of the allegation and to encourage them to make sure parents are aware of all reasonable medical options available to their child. If there is an Infant Care Review Committee, it should also review the situation and report its findings. The Office of Children's Protective Services may also ask the hospital to allow them to review medical records, although there is no legislative authority for that request. By implementing this procedure, the State believes itself to be in compliance with federal regulations.[3]

The public debate over handicapped newborn care— not as heated now, but also not resolved—becomes more comprehensible when placed in context. One relevant context is that of the dialogue that had been carried on in the bioethics literature for more than a decade prior to the eruption of these issues in the public forum. A brief review of the contemporary debate over how to treat congenitally handicapped newborns in a morally responsible way reveals two distinct phases in the development—a "medical criteria" phase and a "due process" phase. I will argue that neither approach is adequate on its own but that elements of each, when combined with an attentiveness to the conversations that take place around the birth of an impaired infant, can contribute to constructing moral rationales capable of guiding future practice.

There is an extensive literature on the medical and surgical treatment of handicapped newborns. As accurately as I can ascertain, however, the first mention in modern literature of the moral dimensions of such treatments is to be found in British journals in the late 1960s. Here one finds positions being taken, as for example in a 1968 paper in *The Lancet*, "Ethical and Social Aspects of Treatment of Spina Bifida,"[4] wherein Sheffield surgeon R. B. Zachary discusses the impact of the birth of a child with spina bifida on families and communities but blinks at the ethical quandaries by asserting categorically that of the options available—to kill, to let die, or to "encourage to live"—only the last is conscionable.

A few years later, a new element emerged, in an issue of *Developmental Medicine and Child Neurology* that carried the first of John Lorber's published attempts to demonstrate that "selection for treatment can be made on an humanitarian basis."[5] Editor R. C. MacKeith noted, "If our present powers of prediction and treatment are inadequate to decide the 'best' policy, so too are our ethical attitudes. Many of us have not faced and thought out attitudes to these problems of life and death. Controlled trials which must continue in different centres should not forget that moral decisions must be discussed and made."[6] These remarks quietly signaled the beginning of a debate that continues to this day about how to treat handicapped newborns.

Lorber's view was bold and controversial. Concentrating exclusively on children with spina bifida and adhering to the principle of the best interests of such children, Lorber developed a short list of medical criteria that together constituted "contra-indications to active therapy." Strict application of these criteria would result, he believed, in a "least bad solution" to a desperate problem. Newborns with severest anomalies would mercifully be allowed to die while maximum therapeutic efforts would be directed toward those children whose chances of benefiting from treatment were good.[7]

The flaw in this otherwise honorable view is the expectation that the newborns selected out would die quickly. That expectation is groundless, and for those infants who do survive, the quality of survival "is poorer than if they had had early, vigorous—optimal—treatment." These were the observations of John Freeman who asked, "Is there a right to die–quickly?"[8] Once we acknowledge that selecting out patients who will receive no treatment is tantamount to selecting them for death, ought we not mitigate their misery by hastening their dying? Dr. Freeman's answer, in a 1974 paper on ethical dilemmas in treating infants with a meningomyelocele was an ambivalent "no." "Active euthanasia might be the most humane course for the *most severely* affected whom you elect not to treat, but it is illegal. 'Passive euthanasia' in which the physician provides less than optimal treatment and therapy and waits for 'nature to take its course' is legal, but in many cases is hardly humane. Therefore, in an *ambivalent* fashion, I feel that *virtually* every child should be given optimal vigorous therapy."[9] In any case, Freeman argued elsewhere, partial treatment is never defensible.[10] Lorber concurred.[11]

Drs. Lorber and Freeman were one in their desire to act in the best interest of these newborns. They disagreed only over how to act responsibly toward the most severely afflicted. Meanwhile, the scope of the discussion was expanding to include the morality of treating or not treating other congenitally impaired newborns. And, with the publication of a landmark report by Raymond F. Duff and A. G. M. Campbell in late 1973, the focus on criteria gave way to a broad-gauged consideration of "moral and ethical dilemmas in the special-care nursery."[12]

In their report, and in subsequent publications, Duff and Campbell made a case for ample parental discretion in deciding the care of impaired newborns. "Living with the handicapped is clearly a family affair," they argued. "We believe the burdens of decisionmaking must be borne by families and their professional advisors because they are the most familiar with the respective situations." Furthermore, decisions for death should be permitted, following careful deliberation on the part of parents and physicians and subject to "suitable medical review."[13]

Responding to increased public attention to the practice of withholding treatment from impaired newborns, John Robertson and Norman Fost[14] reviewed the legality of the practice and argued that if current law was inadequate or inappropriate it should be changed, not ignored. Parents of impaired newborns, though aggrieved, and physicians, no matter how well-meaning, are not above the law. Avowedly alarmed about "the precedent-expanding significance of nontreatment," these authors proposed a process of decision making aimed at minimizing the risk of error and abuse. Such a process might amount to as little as retrospective, selective case review or as much as prospective judicial review. Whatever its form, the intent of the proposal was that of avoiding arbitrariness and maximizing the probability of impartiality in decision making.

Lorber was surely right, that the end toward which all deliberations regarding the treatment of a handicapped newborn should tend is the best interest of that infant. But, while these deliberations must *begin* with diagnosis and prognosis, they do not end there. Lorber ascribed inordinate importance to medical criteria in making what are fundamentally moral judgments.[15]

Freeman, too, sought what was best for the individual newborns in his care and was relentless in pressing the logic of actively ending the lives of those infants with meningomyeloceles who would not be operated on because of their grim prognosis. But faced with a choice between the illegality of active euthanasia and the inhumanity of passive euthanasia, he elected to live with the ambivalence of providing vigorous therapy for *"virtually* every child."

Lorber and Freeman agreed that while parents should be party to decisions regarding the care of their children, in Freeman's formulation, "The only person capable of fully understanding the consequences of each decision is the physician . . . ." This is because the physician has the benefit of long-term experience in treating children with, in this instance, spina bifida. And on the negative side, under the stressful circumstances, "The parents' decision will be primarily an emotional one."[16] (I will return in a moment to the question whether strong feeling detracts from making such judgments.)

There is wisdom in the view articulated by Duff and Campbell that "There is a need in our society for a policy of deciding care according to individual situations as the *parties most involved feel* is correct."[17] But as they acknowledge, their view presumes not only that parents mean their newborn child well, but also that they will act in the child's best interest. In reply to a criticism that such a presumption leaves the door open to parental arbitrariness, Duff and Campbell weakly reply that the policy they advocate "implies trust in people,"[18] and people are fallible.

Robertson and Fost argue persuasively that although the presence in some newborns of anomalies incompatible with life may be sufficient warrant for a decision not to treat, "It does not follow that parents and physicians should *always* be free to decide whether all defective infants should live or die." But these authors question the ability of physicians and parents to make "a socially justified choice" *because* physicians and parents are so deeply implicated in the situation, bound and biased by their particular perspectives. Here is the question of impartiality and objectivity in slightly different form.[19]

If medical criteria provide a necessary but inadequate basis for responsibly deciding how to care for impaired newborns, and if honest differences obtain among experienced physicians regarding parents' ability to understand the condition of their handicapped newborn child and the consequences of decisions made on that child's behalf, where should we turn? We should, in my view, turn to the shaping of traditions of care.

Tradition is the vehicle of collective memory. In the context of this discussion, I mean by tradition, first a *sense* of the kind of care we are giving, a self-consciousness about that care that will prompt an awareness of its contours. One of the side effects of taking cognizance of a thing is awkwardness. An accomplished dancer knows that when the mind focuses on a movement in mid-execution, clumsiness ensues. Such clumsiness is the price of perfecting the movement. Viewed that way, it is an opportunity. I imagine that much of the recent awkwardness surrounding the care of impaired newborns is promising in just this way. In stopping to scrutinize what we are doing, we temporarily sacrifice some fluidity of action for the sake of a better *sense* of what we are about.

Once we have a grasp on the kind of care we are giving, we will be in a position to affirm or alter our actions and to perpetuate critically accumulated experience. "Here is how we have acted in like situations in the past and these are the grounds on which we acted. They continue to commend themselves in that they express values that we hold dear." Or, alternatively, "They require adjustment in light of the undesirable outcome they precipitated." And so on.

To articulate and cultivate collective memory about the care of handicapped newborns is admittedly a tall order. Because such cases are usually hedged about by a poignant urgency, discussions quickly reduce to pragmatic considerations. The chief contribution of ethics to these discussions to-date—moving them beyond What should be done? to Who should do it? and, According to what principles should it be done?—though important, stops short of completing the task at hand. Granted, the task in the heat of the fray is to decide what to do with a particular baby in a specific time and place. But beyond the fray, and prior to it, which is to say now, and most of the time, the underlying question is not What should we do?, but How should we *be*?

The latter question leads inexorably to a consideration of character. This is notoriously slippery terrain. But surely it is possible to speak of character in relation to morality while avoiding the pitfalls of moralizing. What sorts of people do we want taking care of impaired newborns? Compassionate people, surely, with the gift and the willingness imaginatively to enter the world of a stricken family. Decisive people—able to make hard decisions and to act on them. Thoughtful—able to elicit and entertain the views of others and to appreciate complexity. Acquainted with suffering—with the ways it may be borne and the ways it can destroy—and skilled at communicating those ways to someone who is suffering in just this way for the very first time.

"What should we do?" generates a consideration of obligations and sets us thinking about *principles*. "How should we be?" prompts reflections on virtuous action and directs our attention to *persons*. When ethics neglects to ask the latter question, it uncritically accepts medicine's way of stating the matter, adds a level of discourse to the process of decision making (by asking about criteria authority) thereby arguably making the process more rational but missing the moral question: What is good, or least bad? What, in the view of the particularities of a given situation, is commendable?

In his probing investigation into the nature of responsibility, Hans Jonas wrote, "Ethics has an objective side and a subjective side, the one having to do with reason, the other with emotion. The two sides are mutually complementary and both are integral to ethics."[20] My own reading of the recent debate about how to treat handicapped newborns is that it focused almost exclusively on issues of formal responsibility; in other words, on accountability to criteria and rules and procedures, to the virtual exclusion of considerations of material responsibility, that is, of the "content" of responsibility. If Jonas is correct about the necessary complementarity of reason and emotion in ethics (and I think he is), then the imbalance toward "process" must be redressed in order for the dialogue to advance.

It goes without saying that in the absence of rules of right action and warrants for those rules, arbitrariness may prevail. This is the source of the inadequacy of Duff and Campbell's plea for parental discretion unbounded by formal norms of conduct. It is also the case, however (and this went widely unremarked in the recent debate), that absent emotion, absent sentiment, principles and standards are lifeless skeletons. As Jonas puts it, "Without our being, at least by disposition, responsive to the call of duty in terms of feeling, the most cogent demonstration of its right, even when compelling theoretical assent, would be powerless to make it a motivating force."[21] This is the source of the inadequacy of Robertson and Fost's commitment to due process. One can abide by the rules and still miss the moral mark. Granted, Robertson and Fost do not proffer due process as an infallible guide. Nonetheless, they imply that being procedurally scrupulous is tantamount to right moral conduct, to acting aright. But this is no more than a start. Or, remembering Jonas, it is only half the story—the objective half, reason's half.

Before taking issue with this preference for procedure (and the consequent neutralizing of sentiment), let me emphasize that at the level of review, I believe due process to be essential to the kind of decision making under consideration here. It is a necessary hedge against ignorance and an obstacle to self-interest. Its "public" nature and its orderliness are its chief virtues. I have in mind nothing more elaborate than a small group of informed people who might be constituted randomly but regularly to review decisions about the course of treatment, including, but not limited to, decisions for death, and who might act as a sounding board to parents and doctors when differences arise over the course treatment should take. Such a group would serve the limited but useful function of encouraging the thoughtful consideration of not only all data relevant to a case but also the best interest of the newborn as that interest is perceived by everyone responsible for his care and his fate. The authority of the group would be advisory, its mode of operation deliberative, its purpose to clarify and illuminate the ethical dimensions of the case.[22] Finally, as Peter Williams has argued with regard to Institutional Review Boards,[23] the symbolic value of such review should not be underestimated. By constituting such a group, a hospital or a medical school makes a public, good faith declaration that it is concerned with the ethics of caring for handicapped newborns. Disinterestedness—the temporary suspension of commitment to a particular outcome—encourages impartiality. This is essential at the level of review. In the informal give-and-take between doctors and parents, however, it may be a hindrance. Let me explain by returning to the recent debate.

By 1981, the debate had grown shrill and unproductive. It was stymied in a standoff between those who believed handicapped newborns would be best served by parents and doctors making individual determinations by their own lights and others who believed such infants would fare better morally with doctors, consultation committees, and courts following established public procedures.[24] A good deal of carping about moral entrepreneurship was heard on both sides. The only agreement (and that went unnoticed, or, in any event, unspoken) was on the centrality of issues of formal responsibility—reason's half of the story. Meanwhile, the political events recounted earlier were overtaking the debate.

Lost in the increasingly acrimonious shuffle was a valuable, if arguable, insight. Duff and Campbell had voiced their conviction, noted earlier, that

"There is a need in our society for a policy of deciding care according to individual situations as the *parties most involved feel* is correct." I have already discussed the problematic nature of such a view in the absence of provisions for formal responsibility. But, once accountability is ensured, what is the place of sentiment in decisions about proper treatment of handicapped newborns? Disinterestedness is an essential precondition to proper *review* of decision making, but at the bedside it is misplaced. There one expects profound feeling, not a stiff upper lip.

Medicine teaches mistrust of emotion. The presumption is that strong feeling muddles the mind, that emotions are unruly, and that thinking is orderly. It is a questionable presumption, but who would deny the unlikelihood of being able to act competently, not to mention responsibly, while being awash in emotion. Nonetheless, there is something inherently suspect about a policy that systematically excludes parents' deep hurt or ambivalence toward their handicapped infant, or that declares them incompetent to decide their child's fate on the ground that they grieve or are of two minds. The challenge, instead, is to find a way to include such feelings by giving them form. Feeling, given articulate form, can inform action.

This is more than a matter of courtesy. It is an expression of regard on the part of physicians toward those in their care that is integral to healing. It is an acknowledgement of the physician's awareness that these parents have been dealt a wounding blow. Beyond that, it is constitutive of sound decision making. I mean that we (parents, initially, families, and then other cultural groupings with which we identify) either accept infants into the human community, ascribe worth ("interests") to them in our very acts of caring for them, or we do not. It is only in the twentieth century that anyone has argued that rescuing all human offspring is a feasible social goal. We fool ourselves when we speak of the best interests of the newborn as though such interests were there to be discovered. We do not discover that interest, we determine it in view of what we take to be the ends and purposes of being human. And because in our culture, at this historic moment, there are many versions of those ends and purposes, parents of a handicapped newborn must be centrally included, feelings and all, in decisions regarding the fate of their child.

In my own experience, parents of impaired newborn infants are not, in the main, incapacitated by their grief. They express disbelief. They are distraught. They are deeply saddened, and sometimes confused, but rarely incapacitated. This is borne out by such recorded experiences as the account by Paul Bridge and Marlys Bridge in "The Brief Life and Death of Christopher Bridge."[25]

Shortly after his premature birth, Christopher displayed symptoms of what was diagnosed as "possible viral meningitis." After thirty-three days in intensive care, Christopher's condition was stable but poor.

> He had poor reflexes, poor muscle tone, and frequent convulsions. At this time his long term outlook was thought to include severe mental retardation, possible continuing uncontrollable convulsions, possible deafness, possible blindness, possible cerebral palsy, and motor defects that might be extensive enough to make him quadriplegic. Brain damage was believed to be generalized and was thought to involve the cortex.

The pediatrician discussed with the parents the possibility of allowing Christopher to die. They did not fault him for raising the issue, although they admit that it shocked and angered them initially. They very much wanted to be part of the decision making but felt they had too little information on which to base a sound judgment. With one exception, their requests to see Christopher's hospital records were denied. The Bridges felt frustrated by these refusals. The pediatrician felt pressed by their persistence. The upshot was a strained relationship.

> We raise the issue of a tense doctor-patient relationship not because we feel that anything sinister or underhanded was taking place, but because we believe it is relevant in any discussion concerning withdrawal of treatment. A difficult relationship with the pediatrician makes it exceedingly hard for parents to accept without question the pediatrician's recommendation. Indeed, given the best of relationships, we wonder whether parents wouldn't seriously question the recommendation. It's not that people automatically question the advice or motives of physicians. It's simply that in a life-and-death situation we, as parents, want to be absolutely sure that what is being proposed is in the child's best interests. That is why we desired access to the medical records.

Although one must be careful about generalizing from a first-person account, the instructive value of such a story lies precisely in its particularity. Here are parents who, by their own account, although traumatized by their experience, did not fold in the face of pathos. Their misery did not render them incompetent. On the contrary, it informed the decisions they made.

Their personal experience, although particular, is not idiosyncratic. It is corroborated by sociological studies comparing parents' perspectives with physicians' perspectives on the birth of handicapped newborns. I am thinking here, for example, of the interviews done by Rosalyn Benjamin Darling of pediatricians and of parents of children, ages three weeks to nineteen years, with a variety of congenital handicaps.[26] Darling discovered patterns of agreement among the parents interviewed and broad consensus among the pediatricians but a marked disparateness of views between the two groups. "It's hard to find much happiness in this area," one physician is reported as saying, echoing a view that Darling says was repeated in so many words by all the physicians she interviewed. "The subject of deformed children is depressing . . . I can't come up with anything satisfying about it, I can't think of anything good it does. It's not fun or pleasant, it's somebody's tragedy . . . birth defects are roaring tragedies." The parents contacted felt differently. They were by no means uniformly happy with their lot but all were reconciled. Darling describes the prevailing attitude among them as one of "realistic acceptance." She writes, "Many candidly admitted that, if given a choice, they would not have wanted their children to have been born . . . All the parents would have preferred a normal child but they were still able to love the defective child they had." We desperately need more such studies and stories of lived experience to complement and leaven our formal analyses and thereby to contribute to the shaping of new traditions for unprecedented tasks.[27]

To recapitulate, what we do is a function of the way we are. And the way we (parents and doctors and nurses) are when faced with the birth of a congenitally handicapped infant is pained and conflicted. This is apparent in our conversations about the child who came instead of the one we had hoped for. It is to the evidence of these conversations that we must attend if we are to do right by handicapped newborns and their parents.

What we hear in those conversations is practical moral discourse, not talk of rights and duties but of feeling and commitment. These are not negotiations, as much of the ethics literature on the subject seems to assume and imply, but conversations. Negotiations are contractual, conversations personal. Listening long and hard to these conversations, we are likely to discover that the views expressed therein are not normless or unprincipled. We will also discover the impossibility of deducing from any general norm rules governing all situations of like kind. We must, rather, take the more arduous path of building new traditions out of particular instances of misfortune and suffering.

By tradition I have meant the cultivation of collective memory, and the continuation of critically accumulated experience. This is not to be con-founded with consensus. Consensus requires resolution of difference or acquiescence in a prevailing view. Traditions remain vibrant by thriving on conflict and being changed by it. Because traditions are living things, they cannot be willed into existence. Instead, they come to life in the lives of people acting in particular ways and give guidance as those people take note of their actions, remember them, approve of them, or change them in the light of beliefs about life's purposes, and act that way again. Within the existing broad framework of social mores and legal rules that proscribe infanticide and generally prescribe lenience for parents and doctors who withhold life-prolonging treatment from a severely handicapped newborn, we must discern from the strained conversations between parents and doctors and nurses the values we think dispensable and those we think worth preserving and affirming.[28]

Notes

1. The parents of Baby Doe, a Down's syndrome infant with a surgically correctable digestive tract blockage that prevented normal feeding, had declined consent to operate with the result that the baby died six days after birth.
2. See Thomas H. Murray, "The Final, Anticlimactic Rule on Baby Doe," *Hastings Center Report* (June 1985): 5-9.
3. Information provided by Mary Jane McCarty, Program Specialist, Office of Children's Protective Services, Austin, Texas.
4. R. B. Zachary, "Ethical and Social Aspects of Treatment of Spina Bifida," *The Lancet* (3 August 1968): 274-76.
5. John Lorber, "Results of Treatment of Myelomeningocele," *Developmental Medicine and Child Neurology* 13 (1971): 279-303.
6. Ibid., 277-78.
7. Lorber, "Early Results of Selective Treatment of Spina Bifida Cystica," *British Medical Journal* 4 (27 October 1973): 201-204.
8. John Freeman, "Is There a Right to Die—Quickly?", *The Journal of Pediatrics* 80 (May 1972): 904-905.
9. Freeman, "To Treat or Not to Treat: Ethical Dilemmas of Treating the Infant with a Myelomeningocele," *Clinical Neurosurgery* (1974): 134-46.

10. Freeman, "The Shortsighted Treatment of Myelomeningocele: A Long-Term Case Report," *Pediatrics* 53 (March 1974): 311-13.
11. Lorber, "Selective Treatment of Myelomeningocele: To Treat or Not to Treat?" *Pediatrics* 53 (March 1974): 307-308.
12. Raymond F. Duff and A. G. M. Campbell, "Moral and Ethical Dilemmas in the Special Care Nursery," *New England Journal of Medicine* 289 (1973): 890-93.
13. Duff and Campbell, "On Deciding the Care of Severely Handicapped or Dying Persons: With Particular Reference to Infants," *Pediatrics* 57 (April 1976): 487-93.
14. John Robertson and Norman Fost, "Passive Euthanasia of Defective Newborn Infants: Legal Considerations," *The Journal of Pediatrics* 88 (May 1976): 883-89.
15. See Robert M. Veatch, "The Technical Criteria Fallacy," *Hastings Center Report* (August 1977): 15-16.
16. Freeman, "To Treat or Not . . . ," 141.
17. Duff and Campbell, "On Deciding the Care . . . ," 492.
18. See "Authors' Response to Richard Sherlock's Commentary," *Journal of Medical Ethics* 5 (1979): 141-42. Reference is to Sherlock, "Selective Non-Treatment of Newborns," *Journal of Medical Ethics* 5 (1979): 139-40.
19. Robertson and Fost, "Passive Euthanasia," 887.
20. Hans Jonas, *The Imperative of Responsibility* (Chicago: University of Chicago Press, 1984), 85.
21. Ibid.
22. This is a version of the consultation model in daily use throughout academic medicine. In practical terms, I imagine a roster of consultants, likely to be professionals of all the sorts one finds in large health science centers, qualified by their familiarity with the relevant medical ethical issues and available in groups of three or four to be briefed on a vexing case by parents, doctors, and nurses, and to offer them a considered opinion on it. Such small groups might also convene at regular intervals for retrospective review of ethically difficult cases with attending physicians and staff members.
23. Peter Williams, "Success in Spite of Failure: Why IRB's Falter in Reviewing Risks and Benefits," *IRB: A Review of Human-Subjects Research* 6 (May/June 1984): 1-4.
24. See, for example, Raymond S. Duff, "Counseling Families and Deciding Care of Severely Defective Children: A Way of Coping with 'Medical Vietnam,'" *Pediatrics* 67 (March 1981): 315-20; and Norman Fost, "Counseling Families Who Have a Child with a Severe Congenital

Anomaly," *Pediatrics* 67 (March 1981): 321-24.
25. Paul Bridge and Marlys Bridge, "The Brief Life and Death of Christopher Bridge," *Hastings Center Report* (December 1981): 17-19.
26. Rosalyn Benjamin Darling, "Parents, Physicians, and Spina Bifida," *Hastings Center Report* (August 1977): 10-14.
27. And not only "lived experience," but also such thought-provoking, feeling-forming fictions as Katherine Anne Porter's "He" and Peter Nichols' "Joe Egg." See also Joel E. Frader, "Difficulties in Providing Intensive Care," *Pediatrics* 64 (July 1979): 10-16; and Joel E. Frader and Charles L. Bosk, "Parent Talk at Intensive Care Unit Rounds," *Social Science and Medicine* 15E (1981): 267-74.
28. See Robert A. Burt, "Authorizing Death for Anomalous Newborns," in *Genetics and the Law,* ed. A. Milunsky and G. J. Annas (New York: Plenum Press, 1975), 435-50.

What Does Life Support Support?

Albert R. Jonsen

The question What does life support support? is a daunting one. Given the awesome dimensions of the concept "life," it is difficult to know what sources of evidence to draw upon or what manner of analysis to employ. In the absence of clear directions, the ancient style adopted by preachers (although this essay is not a sermon) might be appropriate: cite a text, relate a parable, and then expatiate somewhat on the meaning of text and parable for human life. Unlike the sermon, whose text and parable preachers select from their Scriptures, the text for this essay comes from a very contemporary source, the *New York Times*; the parable is a story from the most up-to-date critical care unit. The text is a brief letter that appeared as a comment on a piece written several weeks earlier by Judge Irving R. Kaufman of New York:[1]

> As a physician and particularly as a director of a hemodialysis unit, I applaud Judge Irving R. Kaufman's effort to bring the issue of the technological prolongation of life of the terminally ill from the isolation of ethical contemplation to the public arena with a plea for society to institutionalize its moral verdicts by legislation. . . .
>
> . . . [B]oth physicians and families must daily face Judge Kaufman's question: "Under what circumstances may life sustaining therapies be withheld from a severely deformed or terminally ill person?"[2]

The writer, Robert L. Scheer, then makes a rather peculiar statement; this statement is the text for this essay:

> In the absence of a clearly stated instruction from the patient, I cannot stop artificial kidney treatments, regardless of how useless such treatments may have become in saving the patient's life. And, contrary to popular belief, the family of such a patient cannot tell us to stop dialysis or do anything but attest to their knowledge of the patient's previously expressed desires. . . . An answer is urgently needed.

Is it not strange that a physician writes that he feels obliged to continue a treatment "regardless of how useless such treatments may have become"? Is it not strange for anyone to feel obliged to perform the useless? Yet, these words are a striking expression of the paradoxes we presently face in using the technologies generally described as "life support." This paradoxical remark of the letter writer stands, then, as the text for this essay.

A parable is defined as "a short fictitious story used to illustrate a religious or moral lesson." The following parable is short and will illustrate a moral point but is real rather than fictitious. Two years ago, in Moffitt/ Long Hospital, University of California at San Francisco, a young woman lay for sixty-four days in the intensive care unit. She was legally dead from the moment of her admission. She had been legally dead from the time she left the referring hospital in Northern California. Yet for sixty-four days, her bodily processes were maintained in order to bring to viability the fetus in her womb. When she died as the result of a cerebral accident, she was pregnant with a twenty-two-week fetus. At the plea of her husband, and with the agreement of physicians, she was intubated and immediately brought to our hospital, where the most refined and sophisticated techniques were applied to maintain her vital processes until her baby could be safely delivered. A healthy baby, slightly premature, was delivered from a cadaver. The woman who had conceived the infant was not in persistent vegetative condition. She was not in permanent coma. She was literally brain dead, meaning that there was clear neurological evidence that she had lost irreversibly all functions of the brain, including those of the brain stem. That is the legal definition of brain death in the state of California and most states in the union. This is the parable for a moral lesson.

All the medical techniques used to accomplish that feat are the techniques casually referred to as "life support." The ventilator, hemo-dialysis, intravenous alimentation, and hydration are commonly applied to the living to support life. In this case, for most of the time those techniques were used, they were applied to a cadaver. It seems rather inaccurate to talk about life support of a cadaver. The parable obviously illustrates an extreme case. Yet it points out again, just as the text does, some of the paradoxes posed by contemporary technological means of the support of vital processes. In moving from text and parable toward an answer to the question that titles this essay, a brief review of medical history will reveal how this paradoxical situation arose. Each step in the development has been an important and positive one in itself. Yet, taken together, they create a difficult medical and moral problem.

A few readers may recall the Drinker Tank; perhaps a few wise, white-headed physicians actually used one. Such mechanical behemoths lie shrouded in dust in the basement of a hospital here and there. At the beginning of the history of modern life-support techniques is the Drinker Tank. This device, more commonly known as the "iron lung," was a time-cycled negative pressure ventilator: an iron cylinder that enclosed the patient up to the neck. By applying a rhythmic cycle of sub-atmospheric pressure in phase with inspiration, it created a rebound effect that facilitated expiration. This clumsy ancestor of all life support systems was invented by Philip Drinker and Louis Shaw in 1928 to deal with the devastating polio epidemics of that era. At the height of these epidemics in the late 1940s, close to 4,000 patients were treated in this manner annually. Improved understanding of the disease process and of respiratory physiology led to a high rate of success. In a study of 500 acute poliomyelitic respiratory patients, seventy-three percent of the patients became free of the respirator within two years of treatment. Of those, eighty-three percent became respirator free within six months.[3]

In 1953, John H. Gibbon, Jr., performed heart surgery during which the life of the patient was supported entirely by the blood oxygenator that he had painfully developed over the previous quarter century. This heart-lung machine made possible the age of cardiac surgery.[4] During the 1960s much more efficient and sophisticated positive pressure ventilators came into use, giving rise to the modern intensive care unit. At the same time, renal dialysis, which had been pioneered by Willem J. Kolff in the 1940s, became possible on an ongoing basis, due to Belding H. Scribner's invention of the arteriovenous access shunt.[5] During the 1970s great progress was made in perfecting techniques for intravenous alimentation and for hyperalimentation. Finally, the opening years of the eighties saw the first clinical use of implanted mechanical circulatory supports, both the totally implantable artificial heart and the left ventricular device, either of them being used on a temporary or permanent basis.[6]

This very sketchy history, which could have included other devices and other events, shows that when we speak of life support, we describe a technical-physiological interface that enables the delivery of nutrients that are essential for metabolism, allows the elimination of wastes, and provides the mechanical and electrochemical energy to sustain vital activities. Each of these techniques, in and of itself, sustains, or substitutes for, an organ vital to integration of the organism. That is precisely what was done in the case of the young mother at Moffitt/Long Hospital. A chain of machines was put together to provide a technological interface with a physiological process. Each particular process was integrated with other processes, delivering nutrients, eliminating wastes, and providing necessary stimulus for energy.

All of this is marvelous. Patients are alive today, in intensive care and cardiac care and neonatal intensive care units, whose lives are being supported precisely by these means. Many of those patients will not leave the hospital. Many more will leave the hospital and succumb within a fairly short period of time, as recent studies on the mortality and morbidity of patients who have gone through intensive care demonstrate.[7] Many will return home healthy and well. Clearly, these developments are extraordinarily beneficial to many human beings. Why, then, is there a problem? Why does the writer of our opening text have a problem? Why does Judge Kaufman have a problem? And why do we call it an ethical problem?

There are certainly plenty of technical problems with life support. Most of the major techniques have their limitations and their adverse effects. The recent history of the artificial heart demonstrates the range of technical problems that have to be overcome to provide an effective and efficient mechanical circulatory support system. Each implantation shows some new problem that is not precisely anticipated. The problem of emboli, for example, resulting primarily from the structure of the valves in those hearts, was not anticipated in the animal studies, which had suggested that the major problem would be hemolysis. Yet, each clinical experience teaches its lessons. And so it has been with the other major technologies; ventilators advanced from negative to positive pressures, hemodialysis found more efficient routes of access, et cetera.

So each new technology presents new clinical and technological problems; continual improvement and refinement goes on with all of them. But we say that these technologies also pose ethical problems. Indeed, it is commonly suggested that the concern about ethical problems in medicine is stimulated primarily by the advances in medical technology. So, there is a general impression that this enormously positive and quite beneficial development creates ethical problems. It may be useful to be more precise about the nature of these problems: in our civilization, we have gotten very good at defining technical problems and remain fairly primitive in defining ethical ones.

Two features of life support or, better, organ support technology give rise to the ethical question. Both are features not so much of the technology but of its historical development. One is that the technical developments have moved from *partial* support to *total* support. We speak of a "support system." The Drinker Tank was a mechanical device able to exert mechanical pressure sufficient to substitute for the loss of the intercostal musculature. It performed one function only: it moved air in and out. But, as technologies for support of other organs were invented, machine came to be added to machine in tandem. It does little good, for example, to be able to deal with respiratory failure if there is no way to eliminate wastes, should kidneys fail. To the ventilatory support is addeᴅ dialysis and to these, hyperalimentation; the elements of total system, getting essential nutrients in and wastes out, are being assembled. This, in effect, was done in the parable of the cadaver mother.

It is relatively rare that patients end up on total system, although some patients get fairly close to it. Yet, as the steps toward total system are taken in an intensive care unit, signs of concern appear among those responsible for the care of the patient. Intubation is almost routine. When dialysis needs to be added, some questions are raised, and when the need for hyperalimentation arises, people begin to argue. As steps are taken toward total system, the suspicion appears that an ethical problem is brewing. Of course, we must recognize that the total system is not really total. It is only quasi-total. And here we glimpse one of the genuine reasons why we have an ethical problem. The system is quasi-total because we have no direct brain support system. The brain can be perfused by supporting ventilatory and circulatory systems, but that is indirect brain support. When the central nervous system is seriously damaged, particularly in its higher cognitive functions, we have no direct intervention. Thus we confront the sort of patient about whom ethical questions are most frequently raised: one whose heart and lungs and kidneys and circulatory system are being supported but whose cognitive functions are profoundly and permanently destroyed.

The parable of the cadaver mother illustrates this most vividly: it is very obvious that she is no longer a person in the world. Her fetus is being nurtured in a cadaver; had it not been for that intrauterine life, she would have been consigned to the grave. The situation can be slightly changed: a pregnant woman has lost cerebral functions and fits the criteria for persistent vegetative condition. Such a person is not in fact dead, but such a person will never feel any consciousness, will never experience the joy of being a new mother, will never see her child grow. The most famous case of life support in recent times, Karen Ann Quinlan, exemplified the support of a life without consciousness; many of the cases now under review by the courts are of this sort. These are the cases that troubled Judge Kaufman and Dr. Scheer. They should trouble us all. Thus, the fact of quasi-total life support is the first facet of the ethical problem.

The second reason we worry about life support arises from the move from *temporary* support systems to *permanent* support systems. The ancients who remember the Drinker Tank might recall that it was intended for temporary use, although for many unfortunate patients it turned permanent. When we see old photos of vast wards with twenty and thirty people permanently in iron lungs, we forget that its inventors and users hoped that it would supply for temporary loss of muscular power; if respite could be given, the power would, it was hoped, be restored. In fact, by the mid 1950s, only thirteen percent of patients remained dependent two years after initiation of treatment; half of these needed support only at night.[8] The intent to devise a technique for permanent use does not appear until the development of chronic hemodialysis (if we exclude the internal cardiac pacemaker). Now there is mechanical circulatory support, which can be used either on a permanent or temporary basis. It is interesting that the temporary use of the circulatory support devices was almost bypassed to jump into the permanent use. It is almost as if the temporary adjunct to nature has been forgotten in the enthusiasm to build a technological person.

We are now seeing the move from temporary to permanent systems in many situations, such as the use of the ventilator for patients with chronic lung disease or for young people with muscular dystrophy who are put on ventilators permanently at the age of fourteen or fifteen. Once again, however, as in the partial to total move, we recognize that we are not dealing with permanent in the genuine sense, but only of the quasi-permanent. No matter how long support can be provided, a time comes when death conquers even the power of the machine. Yet, with artificial hearts, with ventilators, with other sorts of implanted systems, permanent support to the end of persons' lives seems to many a desirable objective. They will live out those lives with a machine as an intimate part of themselves. We know little about how humans will tolerate the technology-personal interface. Obviously, we have two decades of experience with renal dialysis. Obviously, people will, as they always do, react in unique fashion. Still, I believe we here encounter another reason to think of life support as an ethical problem: we face the fact that there will be people living who are not entirely themselves. Indeed, both in the dimensions of time and space, persons whose lives are supported in this fashion may not be "themselves."

We talk about the maintenance of life; we don't often talk about the maintenance of personhood. It interests me little, indeed, not at all, to be alive as an organism. In such a state, I have no interests. It is enormously interesting for me to be a person. With my history, with my place in life, doing the things I enjoy doing, loving those I love, causing the problems that I like to cause, I live my life. It is the perpetuation of my personhood that interests me; indeed, it is probably my major and perhaps my sole real interest. Life support development or organ support development, however, has led us to the situation in which personhood seems either totally or partially lost, while organic life is maintained. This is, of course, a profound philosophical problem: the very nature of human life and personhood.

The profound philosophical problem, which has been pondered by savants since the beginnings of our culture, need not be answered in full in order to reach some acceptable resolutions of particular problems. During the past decade, many of the perplexing questions about foregoing life support have been addressed by physicians, philosophers, and by the law. The work of the President's Commission for the Study of Ethical Problems in Medicine and Biomedical and Behavioral Research (1979-82) drew the scholarly speculation and the practical suggestions into policy formulations that met widespread approval. Two reports of the commission, in particular, advanced the understanding of ethical issues surrounding life support, *Defining Death* (1981)[9] and *Deciding to Forego Life-Sustaining Treatment* (1983).[10]

Defining Death reviewed the scientific, philosophical, theological, and legal considerations that underlie the determination that death has occurred. The report clarified the criteria for declaring a person dead on the evidence that all functions of the brain had irreversibly ceased. A Uniform Definition of Death Statute was proposed, which has been adopted into law in the majority of states. This action has eliminated the widespread confusion about the term *brain death*, which to some meant permanent loss of consciousness and to others loss of intrinsic organic unity. The Uniform Statute selects the latter as the most appropriate concept for public policy and clinical decision making.[11]

Deciding to Forego Life-Sustaining Treatment reviewed the principles and values involved in the application of various technological means of supporting life. The appropriate use of cardiopulmonary resuscitation and the conditions under which life-sustaining technology might be withheld or withdrawn were examined in detail. In general, the principle of "proportionality" should govern these decisions: the benefits deriving from any intervention should, in the eyes of the patient or those responsible for the patient's well-being, balance the burdens that the patient may have to bear as a result of the treatment. The report analyzed certain clinical situations in the light of this general treatment and concluded that sound justification could support the decision to forego life support. The clearest of those situations are the ones in which intervention would be medically futile, or when a competent patient has refused treatment, or when a patient is deemed to be in a persistent vegetative state.[12]

Nonetheless, despite notable advances in understanding the ethics of life support, the ancient philosophical problem remains. It is not impossible to appreciate that the support of organic life alone, as in the case of brain death, or the support of life in which all signs of consciousness are extinguished imposes no moral obligation. It makes sense, within the values of our culture, to respect the choice of a competent person who dismisses the further attendance of physicians, even if death will result. Yet, the problems posed by the capability of technological support pass beyond these cases. Often, the consciousness of the patient is not extinguished but is diminished or has never matured. Often, the physical experiences of such a patient appear to others to be painful or, at best, uncomfortable, despite solicitous care. Such patients are those about whom we ask the questions raised above: Is quasi-total or quasi-permanent support of continued life an obligation that can be demonstrated to fall on physicians and others responsible for the patient? If life cannot be lived in a fashion that the person, even with profound limitations, finds tolerable, must anyone with technological skills strive to support that life?

The meaning of life is a perennial philosophical question and will not be answered any better by modern bioethicists than by the Greeks, the Medievals or the Enlightenment savants. We do have, however, a dimension of the problem that they did not, namely, life totally or quasi-totally, and permanently, or quasi-permanently, supported by machine. The philosophers may ponder this problem. Yet, we will always return to the intuition that life is supported, not by any machines, however wonderful, but by the personal perception of one's history, by the love of one's family and friends, by engagement, however simple, in the ongoing currents of the social and natural world. Unless our life-support technology can support such life, it is empty of human significance. The bodies of those ravaged by disease must be supported so that they can awake to signs of the human world.

Notes

1. I. R. Kaufman, "Life-and-death Decisions," *New York Times*, op-ed (6 October 1985).
2. R. L. Scheer, "Decisions of Life and Death Require Our Judges' Guidance," *New York Times*, letter to the editor (19 October 1985), 26.
3. J. E. Affeldt et al., "Prognosis for Respiratory Recovery in Severe Poliomyelitis," *Archives of Physical Medicine and Rehabilitation* 38 (1957): 290-95.

4. J. H. Comroe, Jr., *Exploring the Heart: Discoveries in Heart Disease and High Blood Pressure* (New York: W. W. Norton, 1983).

5. B. H. Scribner and C. R. Blagg, "Maintenance Dialysis," in *Human Transplantation*, ed. F. T. Rapaport and J. Dausset (New York: Grune and Stratton, 1968), 80-99.

6. M. W. Shaw, ed., *After Barney Clark: Reflections on the Utah Artificial Heart Program* (Austin: University of Texas Press, 1984).

7. L. P. Myers et al., "What's So Special About Special Care?" *Inquiry* 21 (1984): 113-27.

8. Affeldt et al.

9. President's Commission for the Study of Ethical Problems in Medicine and Biomedical and Behavioral Research, *Defining Death: A Report on the Medical, Legal and Ethical Issues in Determination of Death* (Washington, D.C.: U.S. Government Printing Office, July 1981).

10. President's Commission for the Study of Ethical Problems in Medicine and Biomedical and Behavioral Research, *Deciding to Forego Life-Sustaining Treatment: A Report on the Ethical, Medical, and Legal Issues in Treatment Decisions* (Washington, D.C.: U.S. Government Printing Office, March 1983), 60-89.

11. President's Commission, *Defining Death.*

12. President's Commission, *Deciding to Forego Life-Sustaining Treatment.*

Life and Death Choices:
The Patient's Rights

William J. Winslade

We will all die; about this we have no choice. And many of us will have no choice about when or how we will die, whether from an unexpected illness, a freak accident, or a natural disaster. Others will have choices— unwanted and unpleasant perhaps, but choices nonetheless. Some of those choices concern the *quality* of life, such as when a cancer patient chooses to take a second course of chemotherapy for leukemia; and others affect the *length* of life, such as when a kidney dialysis patient elects to stop dialysis and consequently dies. Difficult, often complex, and painful choices sometimes must be made about matters of life and death.

Not so long ago most persons confronted with a serious or terminal illness did not have an opportunity to make many choices. Patients were passive; physicians made choices for them. Sometimes physicians did not even tell patients their diagnosis; even if the family knew, the patient was often kept in the dark. Some patients who are seriously ill or injured still prefer to rely on physicians not only for advice but also for decision making. However, increasing numbers of patients want more control—more facts, options, opinions, and opportunities for choice. And increasing numbers of physicians—for a variety of reasons—are willing to tell patients the facts and give them choices.

In a July 1984 lecture to the American Hospital Association, pollster Louis Harris noted dramatic changes in public thinking about "the right to die" between 1973 and 1985. Harris reported that

> the number of Americans who feel that a terminally ill patient ought to be able to tell his doctor to let him die rather than to extend his life when no cure is in sight has literally jumped from 62 to 85%. Even more significant is the shift in public attitudes about such a terminally ill patient having the right to tell his doctor to put him out of his misery. Back in 1973, a solid 53-37% majority opposed a patient having that right. But now it has all changed: By 61-36%, a big majority think the patient should have that right. An even higher 80-17% majority favor a family having the right to ask a doctor or hospital to remove all life-support services and let the patient who is in a coma and terminally ill die.

Attitudes of physicians, like those of patients, have also changed considerably in the past decade. Physicians tend to be individualistic; they can appreciate the idea of the patient's right to make his or her own choices. But many physicians believe that patients do not really want such choices—that patients are too ignorant, anxious, passive, or intimidated by illness and by hospitals. To some degree this is true. But legal developments have reinforced individual rights of patients. The law of informed consent to health care has emerged over the past twenty-five years as a pervasive and entrenched legal theory, even if it is sometimes disregarded or short changed in medical practice. The "living will" or "right to die" statutes— now passed in at least thirty-eight states, including Texas—reinforce the right of patients to refuse the use of procedures that artificially prolong life (or the dying process). Well-publicized court cases have gradually persuaded some physicians that some patients really do want to die and not be kept alive only to suffer or to be suspended in the limbo of a persistent vegetative state. The fear of death is real but there are fates worse than death. Marginal life in an intensive care unit is one of them. Many older physicians have been willing to allow patients to die when the physician thinks it is appropriate; many younger physicians are willing to honor their patients' preferences. However, all physicians are uneasy about publicity, media attention, and litigation—quite apart from questions of liability. Some physicians are willing to terminate life support only with the authority of a court order—even if the law does not demand it. However, physicians have begun to recognize patients' rights. Louis Harris points out that when

> we compared the attitudes of both doctors and their patients, the results showed that the patients wanted doctors not to hide any truths from them, to tell them bluntly their chances of living or dying, the chances of alternate forms of treatment working—to level with them completely. Again, we also found patients adamant about having the right to tell their doctor to pull the plug and let them die if that is what they want to do. For their part, doctors were somewhat less convinced that patients ought to get the unvarnished truth or to know precisely what the probabilities were for various treatments working. But the physicians did share the basic point of view that if the patient wants the plug pulled, then doctors should have the power to do it.

Despite changes in the attitudes of patients and physicians and despite legal changes permitting the withdrawal of life-support procedures that provide no therapeutic benefit other than to postpone imminent and inevitable death, patients, families, and professionals are often confused, frustrated, and uncertain about what to do.

Consider the following story reported by the Associated Press on December 24, 1985:

> San Pablo, Calif. (AP)—A man accused of forcing a nurse at gunpoint to disconnect the machines that kept his comatose father alive had promised "not to let him linger," a relative said.
>
> Edward T. Baker held a .38-caliber pistol against the nurse's throat Saturday and told her to shut down his father's life-support systems, said police Detective Larry Hunt. Baker surrendered when he was sure his father was dead.
>
> Baker, booked for investigation of murder, was being held without bail Monday and was to be arraigned Tuesday.
>
> His father, Edward C. Baker, 69, was suffering from cancer of the esophagus. He had been admitted to Brookside Hospital on Nov. 20 and had been in a coma since undergoing surgery Dec. 11, Hunt said.
>
> Velma Brown said her brother-in-law had asked his son "not to let him linger" on life-supporting machines.
>
> The 37-year-old son spent Saturday drinking at the Eagle's Lodge, where he had been an employee, said Mike Carlson, the man's former boss. At about 10 p.m., Baker rose from his chair and said, "I figured out what I'm going to do and I'm going to do it," Carlson said.
>
> Baker entered the intensive-care unit at 10:59 p.m. and kept about a dozen patients and staff members prisoner for 15 minutes, repeating over and over that "he wanted his father to die with dignity," officers said.
>
> He surrendered without a struggle after the life-supporting machines were disconnected and he was certain his father was dead, authorities said.
>
> The hospital's chaplain, the Rev. Palmer Watson, spoke to Baker shortly after he surrendered and said the man

believed he did the right thing.

"He felt the situation was pretty much useless," Watson said. "He begged the doctor that day to let him disconnect the machine. The doctor said he'd have to go through the courts."

"He promised his father he would never let him be kept alive by a machine," Watson said.

A physician can order a life-support unit turned off if the family requests it and if the doctor believes there is no hope for improvement, said hospital spokesman Fraser Felter.

While the police statement referred to the father's condition as "terminal," Felter would say only that the type of ailment involved is fatal "if not treated soon enough." Doctors were to conduct further tests in the next few days, he said.

This story illustrates a series of unfortunate events that appear to be a product of ignorance rather than information, impulsive action rather than rational choice. Although one can understand the feelings of frustration that may have driven Baker's son to act, less drastic and more effective options do exist. In California, where these events happened, as in Texas and many other states, there are already laws and procedures that provide alternative and much more acceptable solutions. I'll now suggest how such a situation could be handled if it had occurred in Texas.

The first thing to do in the midst of a medical crisis is get the facts. Even on the basis of the limited information provided in the news story, note that the patient, Edward C. Baker, was hospitalized for twenty-one days prior to his surgery. We don't know from this news report the degree to which Baker was conscious, alert, and communicative during these twenty-one days prior to the surgery, but we do know that he communicated his desire "not to linger" on life support to his son and his sister-in-law. The news report does not tell us, but let us assume that Baker was told that he had cancer of the esophagus, that he understood, and that he consented to the surgery. Was he also told that he might not recover from the operation and remain unconscious? Even if he was not told, he knew that this was a risk. We don't know what Baker told his physician about his desire not to linger or what his physician may have said to him. But Baker clearly had options, opportunities, and rights that he did not exercise. Let us take a closer look at what they are.

73

In Texas the state legislature passed a law in 1977 called the Texas Natural Death Act, and significantly amended it in 1985. The primary purpose of this law is to permit competent adult patients who are terminally ill to direct their physicians to withhold or withdraw artificial life-sustaining procedures when death is imminent. Thus, before the surgery—and Baker had three weeks before the surgery—he could have been told about the Natural Death Act; discussed it with his physician, family, friends, or even his attorney; and documented his desire not to linger on life support if he did not recover from the surgery. It would not be enough, however, to say only that he did not want to linger. His physician would need to clarify possible outcomes of the surgery—good and bad—and Baker would need to clarify his desires and preferences. For example, Baker might have said that "If I don't recover consciousness after the surgery in, say, ten days, I want you to disconnect the life-support systems." The doctor might explain that it might not be possible to determine that quickly whether a patient will recover. Baker might then reply, "Well, okay, keep trying until you know for sure." Or he might say, "Look, I'm sixty-nine years old and I know that cancer of the esophagus is very serious. I am willing to try the surgery but I don't want prolonged life-support. I don't want to put my body through this even if I am not conscious and I don't want to put my family through prolonged agony." Baker has this right. He can tell his physician what he wants, put it in writing in his own words, or sign a standard form provided for the Texas Natural Death Act. The conversation I have imagined occurring between Baker and his physician is not unreasonable, though it rarely occurs.

Both physicians and patients often avoid such discussions for a variety of reasons. Physicians, perhaps more so than the rest of us, don't like to talk about death and in particular don't like to talk to patients about their death. Physicians are supposed to defeat death and save life. Although physicians have become more realistic about their powers and realize that modern life-support technology can often only prolong life but provide no other therapeutic benefits, they are often reluctant to convey this to their patients. Understandably, they don't want to upset already ill persons, cause unnecessary anxiety, or undermine patients' hope or trust in their physician. However, failure to explore patients' real feelings, fears, and even their fantasies about death may be as damaging or even more harmful than a sensitive but honest attempt to deal openly with risks and consequences of treatment. In this case Baker was already concerned about "lingering." His physician should have dealt with the possible outcomes, Baker's fears, and his preferences.

Not only physicians but also patients are often unwilling to discuss such matters with their physicians. Patients sometimes don't want to bother their doctors, don't want to complain or whine—they want to be "good patients." They also fear their doctors—they will tell their families, nurses, or even the cleaning crews but not their doctors what they think or what they want. Patients must be encouraged to talk to their doctors and be educated about how to do it. There is reciprocal responsibility for ensuring that appropriate communication occurs.

In Texas, a patient like Baker has the option of writing down preferences; in light of the 1985 amendments to the Texas Natural Death Act, desires may also be expressed verbally in the presence of a physician and two witnesses. Thus the law permits and encourages the difficult but significant conversations about patients' preferences concerning the use of life-support technologies. Only if such conversations do occur can respect for patients' choices be realized; if desires are not stated and not clarified it will be difficult to show appropriate respect for the unique human capacity to make self-conscious choices about values and preferences, especially the uniquely personal choices that some can make about their own death and dying.

In Texas, as in California, Baker would have an additional option. He may designate another person to make treatment decisions for him if he is comatose, incompetent, or otherwise mentally or physically incapable of communication. So Baker could have formally and legally named his son as his representative to make treatment decisions for him. Had this been done, his son would not have been so frustrated or so powerless. He would have had the legal authority to carry out his father's preferences. In Texas—where the law goes further than in many other states—even if the Texas Natural Death Act has not been signed or a representative designated, the family, in a specific hierarchy of authority, does have legal authority to make treatment decisions on behalf of incompetent family members.

Thus far I have emphasized the right of the patient to choose whether life-support procedures are to be used and to choose another person as his or her health-care representative. Let us suppose Baker had signed a directive to physicians or had specifically appointed his son as his representative. What would the physicians and the hospital be obligated to do? In the news story the physician told Baker's son that he would have to go through the courts. The hospital spokesperson said that the "physician can order a life-support unit turned off if the family requests it and if the doctor believes there is no hope for improvement." Let us consider both of these possibilities.

Since the famous case of Karen Ann Quinlan in 1976, it has become increasingly clear that many courts will uphold the rights of conscious, competent patients to refuse life support (or any other medical treatment). Courts have also indicated that patients while conscious and competent may express in advance what they prefer in the event that they become incompetent and can no longer communicate their preferences. And in several cases where further treatment was useless except to prolong the dying process or nonconscious organic life, even if the patient was not dying, courts have ruled that life support need not be continued. In the case of Baker, his son could have easily, inexpensively, and rapidly been appointed as his father's guardian or perhaps have obtained a specific court order to have the life support discontinued.

Unfortunately, many people are as intimidated by the legal system as they are by the health-care system. But considering the options chosen by Baker's son, going through the courts certainly seems like a more rational and dignified way to carry out his father's desire. However, the task might have been made easier by the physician and the hospital offering to help with the process. Administrators or attorneys at some hospitals will help families obtain appropriate court orders or even petition the court directly for a court order. At other hospitals, ethics committees or ethics consultants work with hospital administrators, attorneys, and clinicians to help resolve problems that arise in particular cases. Physicians who tell families to go through the courts can do this in a manner that either promotes cooperation or produces conflict. We don't know for sure what happened in Baker's case, but it seems that cooperation and mutual support did not dominate.

Now let us consider what happens without going through the courts. If a family requests that life support be discontinued, it must be something that the patient would have wanted. If no signed statement or directive is available, evidence is needed that this is indeed the patient's preference. Next, it is essential that the family speak with one voice; if disagreement or conflict exists among family members, it must be resolved and consensus achieved before going to physicians and hospital administrators. If the family is in conflict, physicians and administrators are likely to refuse to act for fear of subsequent lawsuits—even if that is not highly probable. False beliefs about risks of legal liability or even litigation pervade the medical community because of the spillover effect of medical malpractice lawsuits. Physicians and administrators are extremely cautious when a family in crisis is also in conflict about treatment of an incompetent family member.

Even when families are in agreement, however, it may not be easy to deal with medical, administrative, and legal issues that arise. To illustrate how complex some situations become, consider a recent case.

Sam (not his real name) was a sixty-year-old man who suffered a serious stroke that left him nearly paralyzed and virtually unable to speak. After his stroke, Sam was taken to a local hospital and was placed in intensive care. The stroke was unexpected and caused great disruption in his family. Sam had three teenaged children from a first marriage and three adult step-children from a second marriage. His natural children lived in his home and the others were nearby. His first wife and second wife were both extremely upset about his condition, as were his children. He also had several siblings, two of whom were physicians.

Sam's wife, Irene, was very concerned that he was helpless and suffering in the intensive care unit. In conversations with Sam's neurologist, it became clear that the neurologist believed that the prognosis, while not absolutely certain, was very poor. The neurologist and Irene were standing near Sam's bed when the neurologist told Irene that he believed that Sam was likely to be ventilator dependent for a long time, perhaps permanently. Irene and the physician had been talking near Sam's bed because they believed that he was unable to hear them or comprehend what they were saying. But just after the neurologist made his prediction, Sam moaned and seemed to shake his head to mean "No, no. . . ."

Irene believed that Sam was trying to communicate that he did not want to be on the ventilator now or in the future. Irene was convinced that Sam had heard the prognosis and wanted his helplessness and suffering to end. Only two weeks before, she and Sam had attended a weekend retreat where they discussed whether, if the situation ever arose, they would want their life prolonged by ventilators or other half-way technologies. Irene knew that Sam shared her belief that such an existence was a life not worth living. Until his stroke Sam had been physically active, vital, and full of life. Now he was paralyzed, mute, and only dimly and occasionally aware of his surroundings. He was not totally unaware, however. He seemed to re-cognize family members and would seem to squeeze their hands in recog-nition. After the incident at his bedside Sam's condition deteriorated and his periods of apparent recognition of persons near him diminished.

After a couple of days Irene began to feel that the neurologist's prognosis was correct. She did not stop wishing that it could be different, but she held out little hope that Sam could recover. She asked the neurologist whether the ventilator could be disconnected. The neurologist agreed that the ventilator was only prolonging Sam's current condition and that it offered no therapeutic benefits. But he was reluctant to disconnect the respirator without consulting the other physicians involved (an internist and a cardiologist). The internist was sympathetic to the request, but he was unwilling to agree unless approval of the hospital administration was obtained. And the cardiologist was less pessimistic about the prognosis than the other two physicians. This professional difference of opinion was conveyed to Irene. She was upset and confused.

The rest of Sam's family had mixed reactions to his illness. Sam's children from his first marriage refused to visit him in the hospital after the first couple of days because they felt that he "was dead already." Irene's children, who were close to Sam, were present not only to be near Sam but also to support Irene. Sam's two physician brothers felt strongly that Irene was correct in her beliefs and that she correctly represented what Sam would want for himself. Although different family members were present at different times, Irene spent nearly all her waking hours at the hospital for several weeks.

When I first met Irene, I suspected from her description of the situation that it would be difficult to arrive at an agreed course of action. I agreed to act as a mediator to try to clarify the situation and to facilitate an agreement on whether the ventilator should be removed. I had a hunch that even an agreement about that would not resolve all the issues.

When I met with Irene and her family I was struck by their warmth and closeness. They were able to talk, touch, and even joke, despite the fact that they were obviously already grieving and in pain. They were sad, angry, frustrated, confused, and troubled, but they were also devoted to Sam and hated to see him suffer what appeared to them to be a fate worse than death.

The hospital administrator, I soon learned, did not share my feelings about the family. Irene and the neurologist told me that the administrator was opposed to the idea of removing the ventilator. He preferred not to discuss the matter any further with the family, but was willing to discuss the situation with me and the neurologist with the understanding that I be the representative of the family. In our discussion it was clear that the administrator was a sincere and sensitive person, but that his style and personality clashed with those of Irene and her family. The administrator felt that the family was precipitous in its desire to have the ventilator disconnected. He recognized the difference of opinion and emotion that can arise in such a situation, but he also disapproved of their style. He was unwilling to proceed any further without legal advice.

After the administrator met with his hospital attorney and a second attorney who was a consultant to the hospital, it was agreed that another meeting would be held. The administrator would not agree, however, to having any of the family members present. I would represent the family, an arrangement they accepted.

At this point Sam had been in the hospital about ten days, and was still in intensive care and respirator dependent. He still showed some recognition of persons in his family, but it was infrequent and short lived.

The meeting arranged by the administrator included the neurologist, internist, and cardiologist, three attorneys for the hospital, the administrator, and me. The night before the meeting the attorneys had drafted two documents, one authorizing the removal of the ventilator, and a second, broader document authorizing the removal of the ventilator or any other life support that the physicians agreed was not medically indicated. At the meeting the administrator strongly opposed the less restricted document and it was agreed, after considerable discussion, that the more limited document would be signed by the physicians and the immediate family members to authorize the physicians to remove the ventilator. This was as far as the administrator was willing to go even though the physicians now agreed that the prognosis was extremely poor. The cardiologist was hesitant, but did not dissent.

As you might have guessed, the ventilator was removed but Sam did not die. The attentiveness of the intensive care nurses, the frequent suctioning of fluids from his lungs, and the skilled use of half-way technologies other than the ventilator kept Sam alive. Further negotiations were required.

Irene considered moving Sam from the hospital to a nearby hospice. But it was thought that this would be a more disruptive move than to allow Sam to remain in the hospital. After more discussions with the family—especially by the physician brothers, the attending physicians, the attorneys, and the administrator—an agreement was finally reached that Sam would be transferred from the ICU to a unit in which he received less aggressive care. He died within a day.

This case demonstrates the dramatic interplay of emotion, uncertainty, personality, law, bureaucracy, morality, and preferences that become intertwined. Throughout my involvement in the case, I did not advocate a particular course of action, but I did seek to facilitate an agreement that would carry out Irene's and her family's preferences on behalf of Sam. This was achieved, but not easily or quickly.

I conducted informal negotiations with the family, the physicians, the administrator, and the attorneys. The nursing staff in the ICU was not neglected and their opinions and feelings were sought and considered. When consensus about the poor prognosis became more firmly established and the clash between the administrator and the family was put aside, it became possible to reach a rational agreement to discontinue the ventilator and later to remove Sam from the ICU.

Would it have made any difference if there had been a Natural Death Act Directive signed by Sam prior to his stroke? Such a directive would have not been legally binding on the physicians, but it would have expressed Sam's desires in a more explicit and formal manner. However, the hospital administrator or the attorney could have argued that even a directive would not have been applicable, at least while Sam was in the intensive care unit, because his death was not imminent. So I do not think that the directive would have, on its own, resulted in removal of the ventilator. And once Sam was removed from the ventilator, the decision to remove him from the intensive care unit was not covered by the directive. Perhaps a more generally worded living will would potentially cover this situation, but even then it would be necessary to interpret the general language of the living will document. Very similar negotiations would have been necessary even if there had been a formal directive written in advance.

In this case a designated health care representative would have added little because the family was already in agreement. However, having such a representative would have been useful if there had been uncertainty or disagreement among the family members either about what the patient would want or about who should speak on his or her behalf. As it was in this case, Irene was clearly recognized as the primary spokesperson for Sam even though she was not a court-appointed legal guardian.

The important point of this unfortunate story is that the patient had *communicated* his personal preferences to his wife who was able, admittedly with considerable difficulty, to carry them out. It might have been helpful if he had *documented* them as well, either with a National Death Act Directive or with a designation of his wife as his health care representative. But neither of these formal procedures is as important as the actual communication in advance that enabled his wife to interpret the incident when Sam seemed to say, "No, no. . . ." This was a sad ending to a man's life, but at least it was possible both to interpret and to pay appropriate respect for his final choice.

Death With Dignity: Patients' Rights and the Texas Hospice Movement

Rebecca Dresser

The 1970s and 80s have been decades of radical change in the U.S. health care system. The hospice movement is one of the most interesting developments to have emerged during this period of change. In Texas and in the nation, people have expressed their dissatisfaction with the depersonalized care that terminally ill patients too frequently receive in hospitals. Part of the response has been to develop hospice care programs that focus on comfort and support for terminally ill patients, instead of intrusive interventions to extend their lives.

I. The Hospice Movement, Past and Present

During the early 1970s, the first hospice programs surfaced in the United States. They had four major goals. The first goal was to improve the quality of life of terminally ill patients, by facing the reality of their terminal illness, by giving them maximum control over their care, and by concentrating on keeping them comfortable, rather than attempting aggressive, intrusive treatment that probably would not significantly prolong their lives. Second, the hospice movement sought to give support not only to patients, but also to their families; the treatment "unit" was the patient and family together. Third, hospices provided the services of an interdisciplinary team, including physicians, social workers, clergy, and volunteers. The fourth aim was to address the psychological, emotional, spiritual, and social needs of patients and their families, and to provide continuity of care, including bereavement services for families after hospice patients died.[1] It was hoped that this alternative approach to caring for dying patients would permit them to face their situations with dignity and a sense of personal worth.

In a recent article, Claire Tehan describes the hospice founders. They were often idealistic, nonmedically trained, and critical of the medical care dying patients customarily received. The original hospices commonly relied on enthusiastic and generous volunteers to administer many of the broad range of services offered to hospice patients and their families. Most served patients in their homes, rather than in separate inpatient facilities. As Tehan points out, these were pioneers with a "missionary spirit": they could show others what care of dying patients could and ought to be.[2]

But the early hospices had many obstacles to overcome to gain acceptance. They had to convince the public, the health-care establishment, and government officials that they could accomplish their goals professionally and reliably. Hospice care evolved toward an increasingly refined approach to symptom control and pain management. Members of the hospice movement spent a great deal of time educating people, especially the many dubious physicians whose cooperation and referrals were necessary to hospice success.[3]

These efforts have succeeded admirably. In a very brief time, hospice has been transformed into a vital component of standard health-care services, widely accepted by the public and health-care professionals, and partially supported by government funds.[4] Over 1,000 hospices are now in existence in the United States. Many are affiliated with hospitals or with home health-care agencies; still others are coalitions of several agencies. About 40 percent are independent, some having their own inpatient facilities.[5]

The U.S. hospice movement arose first in the Northeast. As a result, Texas is believed to have fewer programs than some other states, although precise figures are unavailable. The Texas Hospice Organization is a voluntary group of hospices that have joined together to facilitate information exchange and to improve quality of care. As of Fall 1987, 28 hospices had joined this group.

Between 1980 and 1984, a detailed study was conducted comparing the hospice model of health care with traditional health care of terminally ill patients. The National Hospice Study discovered that hospice patients were significantly less likely to be given diagnostic tests and invasive cancer treatments than were terminally ill patients cared for in other settings. An intriguing aspect of the study is its finding that there was no difference in either the quality or length of life of patients in each group. Patients in hospices with inpatient services, however, were less likely than patients in conventional care settings to experience severe pain and other symptoms. According to the study, patients' families were more satisfied with the care given in hospices with inpatient services than they were with care given either in hospices offering only home care or in conventional care settings. Last, the study determined that costs were significantly less only in hospices with no inpatient facilities; care in hospices with inpatient facilities costs only a little less than conventional care.[6]

Although these results fail to show that hospices are overwhelmingly preferable to conventional care settings, they do indicate that hospice is an option that can offer terminally ill patients and their families satisfactory care at some financial savings.[7] Furthermore, the study's failure to find differences in the quality of life experienced by patients in conventional and hospice settings may simply represent another measure of the hospice movement's success: The hospice philosophy has become integrated into customary hospital care, as indicated by hospitals' increased willingness to offer terminally ill patients a broader range of choices about the treatment and services they receive.

An additional indication of the hospice movement's gains is the 1982 legislation enacted by the U. S. Congress that made hospice care reimbursable through the federal Medicare program. Now patients over 65 with fewer than six months to live may use their Medicare benefits to obtain care from hospices certified by the federal government. To gain federal certification, hospices must offer inpatient care and may not discharge any patients who have been accepted for care. But the federal reimbursement system also has limitations: the average cost per Medicare patient cannot be above $6500, and coverage is limited to 210 days of hospice care for each Medicare patient.[8]

Many states have also enacted licensing laws covering hospices. The federal Medicare reimbursement requirements and state licensing laws will work to make hospice care more uniform. The positive aspect of this phenomenon is that all hospice programs will have to meet certain minimum requirements and standards of care.[9] But increased uniformity also has its drawbacks. Hospice care is becoming more controlled by professionals and is experiencing budgetary and administrative constraints similar to those faced by conventional health-care facilities. As a result, hospice may lose some of its former special characteristics and those hospices that fail to fit the federal and state hospice model may not survive.[10]

II. Ethical Issues

The experience of over a decade of hospice care, together with the evolution over time of the hospice concept, has led to recognition of several ethical issues bearing on hospice care. As Joanne Lynn and Marian Osterweis have described in their excellent survey of ethical issues arising in hospice care, these issues are related to three moral principles: (1) competent patients should be the major decision makers about the medical care they receive; (2) when patients become unable to make their own decisions, those who make choices for them should be guided by the patients' past expressed wishes about treatment or by an assessment of their present best interests; and (3) society should distribute its health-care resources with justice and fairness.[11]

A. Competent and Informed Decision Making

The individual's freedom to make important decisions about her care without improper interference by others is called the right of self-determination. This freedom is highly valued in our society and is supported by longstanding moral and legal principles. The right of self determination includes the freedom to make decisions about one's medical treatment.[12] But because medical treatment decisions of seriously ill patients can involve life, death, and other crucial matters, ethical and legal rules exist to ensure that these decisions meet certain criteria. Before their decisions about treatment will be honored, patients must make decisions voluntarily, without the overbearing influence of others, be sufficiently informed about their illness and the various treatment alternatives available to them, demonstrate an adequate understanding of this information, and supply an explanation of their choices to others.[13] Patients who fulfill these criteria are regarded as competent to make decisions about their health care.

Particular characteristics of the hospice patient, however, can create special problems and challenges in determining whether or not patients are competent. Terminally ill patients often feel that they lack power and control over their lives. As a result, the wishes of other people will sometimes be overly persuasive to the hospice patient.[14] Physicians, health-care professionals, and other hospice workers must take care to give patients freedom to choose, at the same time supplying support and security to patients, so they do not feel abandoned. Hospices are especially suited to helping patients feel less vulnerable, by allowing them greater control over their lives during their illnesses, by increasing their self-esteem through supplying personal attention and counseling, and by providing a less threatening environment than that of the typical hospital.[1]

Patients must also be informed about their conditions and available treatment. As the President's Commission for the Study of Ethical Problems in Medicine stated in a recent report, all health-care professionals, including those working in hospice programs, are obligated to explain to patients

> (1) their current medical status, including its likely course if no treatment is pursued; (2) the interventions that might be helpful to the patient, including a description of the procedures involved and the likelihood and effect of associated risks and benefits; and (3) in most cases, a professional opinion as to the best alternative.[16]

Two matters related to patient decision making can raise special difficulties for hospice patients and workers. First, terminally ill patients eligible for and receiving hospice care may be especially debilitated. Their fatigue and discomfort will sometimes require hospice workers to spend extra time and effort to inform these patients.[17] A second problem hospice workers commonly encounter arises when a patient is referred for hospice care without having been informed of her terminal prognosis. Because hospices are designed specifically to care for terminally ill patients who prefer supportive and palliative care over aggressive treatment, patients should never make the decision to enter hospice without being aware of their prognoses.[18] To ensure that their patients are so informed, one Houston hospice requires patients to sign a consent form stating, "I understand that [this hospice] serves patients who have incurable, life-limiting illnesses, with life expectancy measured in weeks or months."[19]

Patient comprehension and reasoning are additional requirements of competent treatment decision making. Patients should demonstrate to others that they understand information relevant to their decisions and can give reasons for their choices, reasons that reflect their general values and preferences.[20] This demands conversation between hospice workers and patients. The only way hospice workers can assess patients' comprehension is through discussion and exchange; patients must be questioned about what they understand and workers should never simply assume that patients understand everything they are told.[21]

The range of choices available to hospice patients includes the freedom to refuse life-sustaining treatment. If a terminally ill patient's decision against treatment is voluntary, informed, and adequately reasoned, medical ethics and law support the patient's right to refuse such treatment.[22]

The Texas Natural Death Act supports this view by allowing competent patients to direct physicians to withhold or withdraw life-sustaining procedures that would serve only to prolong artificially the moment of death.[23] Qualified patients are those inflicted with incurable illness or injury, which in the physician's reasonable medical judgment will produce death despite the application of life-sustaining procedures. The law provides that treatment directives may be written or oral, and patients can also issue directives naming another person to make treatment decisions for them in the future. All these directives take effect if the patient becomes "comatose, incompetent, or otherwise . . . unable to communicate." The Texas law also allows close relatives of incompetent adult patients, and the parents or spouses of patients under 18, to make directives for these patients. Again, these patients must be incurably ill or injured, with death "imminent" whether or

not life-sustaining procedures are utilized.

Two questions about the meaning of specific provisions in the Texas Natural Death Act may be relevant to the treatment of hospice patients. One concerns how close to death a patient must be to be covered by the law. The requirement that a patient be "terminally" ill and expected to die "imminently" is sufficiently imprecise to create uncertainty in some cases. No Texas court has addressed this question, but in 1986 a Virginia court was asked to interpret provisions in the Virginia Natural Death Act identical to those in the Texas statute. The case concerned a patient with a malignant brain tumor who was expected to die within three months, but might survive for several months. Her family went to court for authorization to remove her gastrostomy feeding tube, in accord with her formerly expressed wishes. The court held that the patient was covered by the Virginia law, noting that if the law only covered patients for whom death was "hours away," there would be no need for a special statute authorizing life-sustaining treatment to be forgone.[24]

The second question that has arisen under the Texas Natural Death Act is whether the law authorizes withholding or withdrawal of medication or medical nutrition and hydration. The life-sustaining procedures that may be forgone under the Act "shall not include the administration of medication or the performance of any medical procedures deemed necessary to provide comfort or care or alleviate pain." Does this provision absolutely exclude medication, nutrition, and hydration, or does it exclude them only if these procedures are administered for comfort or pain relief?

Again, no Texas court has considered this question, but courts in other states offer some guidance. The Virginia case mentioned earlier also addressed this matter, because the Virginia law includes the same definition of life-sustaining procedures. The court held that nutritional support could be withdrawn from the patient because in her case it was being used to supplant a vital function, not to maintain her comfort. (The patient was comatose and her physician testified that she was unable to experience pain.) Another pertinent case arose in Florida, whose Natural Death Act expressly excludes nutritional support from its definition of life-sustaining procedures encompassed by the Act. In 1986, a Florida appellate court held that nutritional support could still be removed from an irreversibly comatose patient, based on the patient's constitutional right to have removed any artificial measures that sustain life.[25]

Although the issue has not been definitively resolved in Texas, court cases in other states suggest that medication and nutritional support may be withheld or withdrawn when they are used solely to extend the biological

lives of terminally ill patients. But there also are limits on the competent patient's "right to die." Terminally ill patients are permitted to refuse further medical interventions. This withholding of treatment is called "passive" euthanasia: the failure to intervene medically to prevent death from an underlying disease or injury. Patients have no right, however, to have hospice workers, families, or friends end their lives by administering lethal injections or otherwise actively killing them, even though this action might constitute the least painful, most merciful alternative.[26] The legal prohibition of active euthanasia rests partially on fear of the slippery slope: if active euthanasia were permitted, too many abuses would inevitably follow. But this is a controversial area, and some "right to die" groups are working to change existing law to allow active euthanasia in certain carefully reviewed situations.[27]

It is also important that we allow terminally ill patients a full range of choices. Recently, the focus has been on their right to refuse treatment, but we must also take care not to deny them the right to obtain the medically acceptable aggressive treatment they might want. Hospice patients sometimes change their minds and want to be hospitalized or try chemotherapy or other potentially life-extending, aggressive treatments they formerly refused.[28] Problems have arisen regarding such decisions, for economic factors can be involved. For example, before a Medicare hospice patient can be admitted to the hospital, a nurse must decide whether the patient's condition is serious enough to merit transfer to an acute-care facility.[29] Another example is that Medicare hospice patients who decide to attempt treatment for their terminal conditions automatically lose hospice benefits for the rest of their entitlement period, which can be as long as three months.[30] These economic constraints on hospice patients' freedom raise questions about the justice and fairness of such requirements, which will be discussed in a subsequent section of this essay.

B. Deciding for Incompetent Patients

A second important ethical issue involves deciding on treatment of hospice patients who cannot make decisions for themselves. These are patients who are unable to understand and reason about treatment alternatives in the way that competent patients can. Some of these patients are unconscious, or conscious but unresponsive, or confused because of their medical conditions or the drugs necessary to treat their conditions. Unfortunately, many terminally ill patients become incompetent, and other people are confronted with the task of making decisions about their care.

The majority of hospice patients are competent when they make the decision to enter hospice care (Medicare patients are *required* to make the initial decision to enter hospice and sign the consent form themselves[31]), but most patients at some point will become unconscious or otherwise unable to make their own treatment choices.

The ethical goals in caring for incompetent patients are to advance their well-being and, if possible, to respect their self-determination rights. The difficulties in meeting these goals arise from the possibility that the values held by the outsiders making decisions for the uncommunicative patient can easily enter into their choices.[32] Living wills and other advance treatment directives can be very helpful in these situations. Texas law enables terminally ill persons to execute a living will or to designate a proxy decision maker in advance.[33] The latter legal mechanism allows people to name the person they want to act as their treatment decision maker if they later become incompetent. They can choose an individual they trust and one with whom they have discussed their personal values and goals.

But what of those many incompetent patients who failed to issue explicit advance instructions through living wills or documents naming their chosen proxy decision makers? As was noted previously, the Texas Natural Death Act permits family members to make treatment decisions on behalf of their terminally ill incompetent relatives. The dominant view in ethics and law is that such proxy decision makers should first attempt to determine whether the patient informally expressed preferences about treatment. If reliable evidence exists concerning a patient's past expressed wishes, that evidence ought to be seriously considered when treatment decisions are made.[34] For patients who made a competent decision to enter hospice care and later became incompetent, the earlier decision to forgo aggressive treatment in favor of the hospice approach stands as an indication of the patient's general treatment views. Hospice workers, family members, and friends can feel comfortable adhering to the same general treatment approach the patient originally chose.

Problems can still develop, however, when family members and hospice workers disagree on the decision that would most respect a patient's right to self-determination or advance his or her well-being. Although we usually assume that family members will know a patient's former beliefs and values and make decisions in the patient's best interests, they sometimes have conflicts of interest that can lead them to place their own preferences above the patient's interests.[35] For example, relatives might want an intervention withheld that care-givers believe the patient would have chosen, if she were still competent. Relatives also may disagree among themselves about the appropriate decision.

Some mechanism is needed to resolve these cases. Institutional ethics committees have become popular in hospitals as a means of resolving difficult ethical issues.[36] Hospices may want to adopt this device or a similar one to address disagreements over treatment of incompetent patients.[37] Ethics committees are typically composed of health-care professionals and a social worker, member of the clergy or ethicist, attorney, and layperson from the community. Their meetings create a forum for discussion. Members supply information associated with their areas of expertise and an element of objectivity in the search for the treatment decision that most advances the incompetent patient's interests. Courts are a last resort for handling intractable treatment disputes, but the time and costs typically consumed by legal proceedings make this a poor mechanism for resolving conflicts about the care of hospice patients.

C. Distribution of Hospice Care

A final major ethical issue concerns who gets hospice care. Are any patients who want hospice care denied it for economic or other reasons? Patients in the United States have no legal right to be admitted to hospice.[38] Individual hospices can decide which patients they will serve. Some programs accept only patients with cancer, excluding persons with other progressive terminal illnesses.[39] Hospices generally restrict their services to patients with prognoses of twelve months or less.[40] Many hospices offer services to adults only; adolescents and children often cannot obtain hospice care unless a special program exists for them.[41] Virtually all hospices require that patients have someone available to care for them in the home.[42] Although some hospices accept patients without regard to their ability to pay, others require that patients have insurance, Medicare, or other financial coverage to compensate for their care.[43] Furthermore, the Medicare reimbursement program has provisions that have encouraged hospices to adopt more stringent criteria than they formerly applied, reducing the range of illnesses accepted and limiting the point at which patients become eligible for hospice care. The law mandates that eligible patients must have 24-hour-a-day home care, and that families must assist in such care.[44] Some observers believe these limits on hospice care are unfair. They ask why the specific diagnosis or family situation of seriously ill persons should determine their eligibility for hospice care.[45] Some argue that hospice care is a treatment option that ought to be available to all terminally or seriously ill patients, because hospice care is part of the adequate minimum of health care society is morally required to make available to everyone.[46] Others disagree, noting that the present availability of other forms of health care for seriously and terminally ill patients makes society's obligation to provide hospice care less pressing than it is concerning other health programs, such as childhood vaccination and emergency medical services.[47]

Hospice availability is essentially an issue to be resolved in the political arena, one of the many "gray area" health-care programs that must compete in the legislative and executive contexts for the limited funds available to increase access to health care.[48] By providing Medicare reimbursement for hospice care, the U.S. Congress has taken one step toward including hospice care as part of the adequate level of health care that should be available to certain patients over age 65. But this recognition is limited, and many other patients who could benefit from hospice care are presently denied it and must instead seek care in hospitals and nursing homes.[49]

Conclusion

There is no doubt that the hospice movement has expanded terminally ill patients' choices. Hospice is one component of our recent cultural awareness that we need not always bow to the "technological imperative," which holds that if something can be done, it must. Nevertheless, hospice and its underlying philosophy are not a panacea. Many ethical dilemmas remain in the care of terminally and seriously ill persons, such as the challenges of (1) protecting the competent patient's freedom to choose from among a variety of health-care options; (2) protecting the interests of incompetent patients; and (3) distributing hospice care benefits to patients according to ethically defensible admission criteria. These are among the challenges the hospice movement will face in its new phase as a valued component of today's accepted health-care services.

Notes

1. Claire Tehan, "Has Success Spoiled Hospice?", *Hastings Center Report* (October 1985): 10. See also J. Robertson, *The Rights of the Critically Ill* (1983), 155; President's Commission for the Study of Ethical Problems in Medicine and Biomedical and Behavioral Research, *Deciding to Forego Life-Sustaining Treatment* (1983), 112-13 [hereafter cited as *Foregoing Life-Sustaining Treatment*].
2. Tehan, 10.

3. Ibid. See also Greer and Mor, "How Medicare is Altering the Hospice Movement," *Hastings Center Report* (October 1985): 5, 8.
4. Tehan, 11.
5. Greer and Mor, 6.
6. Ibid., 5-6.
7. Ibid., 6.
8. Ibid., 5. See also *Foregoing Life-Sustaining Treatment*, 115-16.
9. Robertson, 159.
10. Tehan, 11.
11. See Lynn and Osterweis, "Ethical Issues Arising in Hospice Care," in *Hospice Programs and Public Policy*, ed. P. Torrens (1985), 199-200, 210. See also *Foregoing Life-Sustaining Treatment*, 26-27.
12. *Foregoing Life-Sustaining Treatment*, 44.
13. Ibid., 45-60.
14. Lynn and Osterweis, 205-206.
15. Ibid., 209; Robertson, 155.
16. *Foregoing Life-Sustaining Treatment*, 51-52.
17. Lynn and Osterweis, 207.
18. *Foregoing Life-Sustaining Treatment*, 114.
19. Consent form, New Age Hospice, Houston, Texas.
20. Lynn and Osterweis, 208.
21. *Foregoing Life-Sustaining Treatment*, 56-60.
22. Ibid., 89-90. See also Robertson, 32-47.
23. Tex. Health Code Ann. tit. 71, art. 4590h (1985).
24. Hazelton v. Powhatan, No. 98287 (Va. Cir. Ct., Fairfax County, 29 August 1986). affirmed, No. 860814 (Va. Supreme Ct., 2 September 1986).
25. Corbett v. D'Allesandro, 487 So. 2d 368 (Fla. Dist. Ct. App.), review denied, 492 So. 2d 1331 (Fla. 1986).
26. *Foregoing Life-Sustaining Treatment*, 65-73.
27. "Physician Aid-in-Dying Law," *Hemlock Quarterly* (January 1986): 1-8.
28. *Foregoing Life-Sustaining Treatment*, 114-15; Robertson, 157-58.
29. Tehan, 11-12.
30. Lynn and Osterweis, 206.
31. Ibid., 211.
32. Ibid., 210.
33. Tex. Health Code Ann. tit. 71, art. 4590h (1985).
34. *Foregoing Life-Sustaining Treatment*, 132-34.
35. Ibid., 127-29.
36. Ibid., 160-70.

37. Lynn and Osterweis, 211.
38. Robertson, 156.
39. Ibid.
40. Lynn and Osterweis, 213.
41. Robertson, 156.
42. Lynn and Osterweis, 213.
43. Tehan, 11.
44. See L. Paradis, *Hospice Handbook: A Guide for Managers and Planners* (1985), 4.
45. Lynn and Osterweis, 214-15.
46. Ibid., 214-15.
47. Ibid., 212.
48. Ibid. See also President's Commission for the Study of Ethical Problems in Medicine and Biomedical and Behavioral Research, *Securing Access to Health Care* (1983), 36.
49. *Foregoing Life-Sustaining Treatment*, 115-16.

Death & Age:
A Natural Connection?

Sally A. Gadow

Old age is unique among the stages of life: it is increasingly regarded as the natural time to die. Death is resisted less vigorously (if at all) in older persons, while the death of a child is considered a violation of the natural order. Chekhov's character Iona mourns, "Here my son is dead and I am alive . . . death has come in at the wrong door."[1] The view that advanced age is the right door for death makes the elderly the only group for whom death is culturally accepted. Is that view a form of privilege reserved for the aging, analogous perhaps to the advantages that hospice personnel, with their special openness toward death, offer the dying? Or is it a form of discrimination, a subtle version of the prevalent denigration of aging? The question, in short, is the ethical issue that lies at the heart of all social and medical approaches to aging: to what extent and to what ends should old age be viewed as the natural time to die?

The consequences of accepting a natural connection between death and age are troubling. Designating death in late age as more natural than earlier death may not mean forcing elderly patients to die by denying them care, but it may encourage them, through the governing ethos, to regard their own deaths as natural and so to refuse care. Granting persons the right to die on their own terms is, in most views, an advance over deciding for them when they will die. But identifying *types* of death as acceptable is morally more problematic. "The right to die becomes transformed into the obligation to die, by which elderly people are persuaded to join as agents in their own social devaluation and, consequently, in their own physical destruction."[2]

Because the concept of "natural" carries such moral weight in the current context of life-ending decisions, we must examine the concept's meanings critically. In what sense might death be viewed as natural? Specifically, in what sense can death in old age be considered natural? In the discussion that follows, I analyze three common meanings: death as inevitable, death as it occurs in nature, and death as peaceful. I then offer and defend an alternative interpretation.

Death as Inevitable

Before this century's advances in health care, death was apt to occur at any age, especially infancy. Now, we place death in what we consider its normal position, at the close of a long life.[3] Indeed, successes in preventing or treating a myriad of hitherto fatal conditions have bred the hope that all deaths are preventable—all, that is, except the one at the end of a long life. But the explosion of longevity research suggests that even the timing of *that* death is debatable: the end of life may be later than we think. The natural time for death so far is negotiable: death at ninety may become as preventable as death in infancy. The claim that death is natural after a long life assumes the possibility of agreement on "long enough," and that agreement is not yet available, at least on the abstract level of lifespan for the species. On the concrete level, applying the lifespan meaning of *natural* to an individual life ("Has this woman lived as long as it is possible for her to live?") is equally inconclusive, since death can be almost indefinitely delayed and there are no grounds for conceding its inevitability until it has finally (irreversibly) occurred.

The question of when a particular life has lasted long enough *can* be answered, but not on the basis of species lifespan or clinical prognosis. The question is answerable only on the basis of personal criteria for fulfillment. Since individual fulfillment is a subjective achievement not amenable to quantitative measurement, those criteria have no necessary connection to age. The common equating of chronologically long life and long-enough life is a confusion of those two measures and fails to distinguish between the quantitative and the personal, the external and the individual. When death is categorized as natural after a long life, that claim must be understood as a strictly external perspective based on abstract survival estimates, with no intrinsic bearing on personal measures of "long enough."

Death as in Nature

A different meaning of *natural* reflects the belief that death is acceptable, not when it is inevitable, but when it follows the model of death in nature. One living will expresses the view poetically: "Death for an older person should be a beautiful event . . . What is more beautiful than the spring budding of small leaves; the fully-leaved tree in summer; the brightly colored autumn leaves gliding gracefully to the ground?" If death itself is not a violation of the natural order, the sentimentalizing of nature surely is. That leaves must fall, we accept. But that the living tree be felled? That the fawn be fed to the wolf? That the foot be eaten by gangrene? Death in nature, anthropomorphically speaking, is violent and appalling. The only alternative nature offers its creatures is an unconscious death, "the frozen sparrow under the hedge, the dead leaf whirled away before the night wind."[4] Where is the death in nature that we would wish for ourselves at any age? A related meaning of *natural* is based on the way creatures in the wild do *not* die; that is, never do they die in intensive care units. Human dying modeled on this aspect of nature is marked by freedom from intervention. But how much intervention must be eliminated to make a death natural? Basic technology, such as intravenous feeding? Only high technology such as respirators? Only *heroic* high technology such as that used for heart transplantation? Or literally all intervention (thus, conceivably, a refusal even to place food within reach of bedfast patients who could feed themselves)? In principle, any intervention can be viewed as unnatural, even when nothing overtly artificial, like apparatus, is used. An absolute line between natural and artificial is impossible to draw. Even nature obscures the distinction. Creatures intervene to alleviate one another's suffering and delay death: a community of dolphins will support an ailing member at the water's surface to keep it from sinking and drowning.

Nature itself provides us with no humanly ideal manner of dying, nor does it help us distinguish natural from artificial—if by "natural" we want to mean "nonartificial." Nature does help, however, in a different way. It provides a model for justifying death. "All of the life of the earth dies, all of the time, in the same volume as the new life that dazzles us each morning, each spring."[5] More precisely, all of the life of the earth dies in order to make way for the same volume of new. Nature produces a virtual infinity of life forms, but only so long as none of the lives lasts indefinitely, usurping the place of its successor. The naturalness of death in old age may poetically connote idyllic beauty or freedom from technology, but the only straightforward connection with nature is neither of those meanings. The connection comes, rather, from the ecological view of death; life is wasted on creatures past their ability to support new life. Their continued life is in fact worse than wasteful—it endangers the new. In short, the only sense of natural death that can be wrested from nature itself is that the old die for the sake of the young.

In the human species, ecological death translates into economic values. "Costs may make it appropriate to give insurance discounts for those who enact a living will. One might envisage Medicare requiring all recipients at least to review a living will."[6] For the elderly, the destructive implications of the concept of ecologically natural death are too obvious to need comment. One point, however, should be emphasized. No matter how vigorously that meaning of natural may be denied, as long as the aging are distinguished as the special group for whom acceptance of death is reserved, they never can dismiss entirely the possibility that they are invited to die for the sake of their successors.

Barring the ecological meaning, it becomes clear that the naturalness of death has nothing directly to do with nature. The term *natural* is not even a metaphor for an identifiable aspect of nature; the term serves a more generic function—to evoke the special sentiment that an industrialized culture cultivates with respect to that part of the world from which it feels most removed. Given the powerful symbolic value that modern sentiment projects onto the natural world, the association of human dying with nature has an almost irresistible appeal. Despite our failure to identify exactly what it is about wild creatures' dying that is "natural," the association of human death with nature nonetheless imbues death with the same compelling mystique that has come to surround nature itself.

Death as Peaceful

The ideology surrounding nature includes biology. Even if the conscious experience of dying finds no model in nature, beneath consciousness cells age and die according to biological laws that rule throughout nature. Scientifically, a natural death is a lawful death, a reasonable, intelligible dying, orderly and peaceful, neither pathological nor violent.

The ideal of a peaceful death is the most subtle of the associations between human dying and nature. On the surface, the connection is not obvious, since death in the wild often is brutal by human standards. The connection is conceptual rather than visible. The key is the concept of death as biologically foreshadowed in aging, or (the same concept from the other side) aging as organic preparation for death. "Death is embodied in decrepitude."[7] Aging, biologically speaking, is dying.

The subtlety of this view is that the weight of "natural" shifts from death to aging, and from the experience of aging to the physiology of aging. Natural aging is progressive demise, interrupted in some cases by violent pathologies such as stroke or heart attack, but in principle peaceful, an orderly deconstruction of the organism. "Dying of old age" epitomizes death as the normal culmination of an internal necessity, an image sharply contrasted with the death, for example, of a child hit by a car, a death violent in two senses: first, caused by an external force, one that cannot by any reasoning be considered intrinsic to the being of the child; second, caused by a force so overwhelming that destruction is total and immediate, neither gradual nor gentle. If peaceful death has a biological model in aging, then such a doubly violent death is unnatural in yet a third sense. It occurs outside aging, for only in aging is death the fulfillment rather than the violation of a normal biological impetus.

In the image of an easy, gentle death as the extension of aging, natural turns out to have no meaning at all. The claim that death is natural in aging becomes a tautology when death already has been designated as the telos of aging. The convenience of the view is its scientific reinforcement of an ideal that has many advocates, the image of the good death as one that is peaceful. But the price of a biological model for that ideal is the equating of aging with destruction. Although the cost to the elderly may not be as high as in an ecological view of death, it may nevertheless be too high. Aging persons are not literally sacrificed for the good of the culture, but their experience is sacrificed to the "good death" their culture idealizes. The freedom to understand their own aging in personal ways is usurped by an official biological interpretation. But aging is more than the process of cells dying, just as death is more than the sum of their dying. Aging and death are two of the biological phenomena for which every culture and individual must establish meanings. "Biological" cannot count as one of those meanings, since it itself requires interpretation in order to have a place with the rest of human reality. If we choose to use biological processes as the model for an experience such as aging, their meaning there is metaphorical, not definitive. Neither the dying of cells nor the dying of dolphins signifies anything relevant for human experience until a decision is made to adopt one or the other as an ideal and thereby infuse it with symbolic value.

An Alternative

All of the views of death in aging discussed above share a common misunderstanding. They assume a discoverable realm of phenomena not constituted by human meanings, a natural realm that transcends human ambiguities and artifice. That world, where creatures live unsullied by human yearnings, is complete and intact, independent of human interaction, untouched by moral turmoil or existential quandary. The positing of such a realm means that "nature itself has become a new deity. Nature harmonizes, nature orders, nature provides us with a rule of life."[8] Appeal to a natural realm rescues us from the maze of human relativity because the referents for meaning that it offers—laws of physiology, animal behavior, the earth's seasonal cycles—are not themselves the product of human contrivance.

But the conception of a separate natural realm *is* a human contrivance, as analysis of the three views has tried to show. Nature is intelligible only through human interpretation. The historical flux of scientific paradigms is reminder enough that the natural is not a realm we can know without benefit of humanly designed constructs, theories, and values. To the extent that it is knowable only through human understanding, nature—like human experience itself—is an edifice of human construction, not a free-standing, self-revelatory world.

The impulse to refer to the natural in making sense of human aging and dying is an expression of the most basic moral impulse, the attempt to understand experience in light of an ideal. Fashioning a view of the good in naturalist terms becomes pernicious only if the essentially human meaning of natural is suppressed. That suppression is hard to avoid when the very concept of nature as "other" obscures the fact that ideals found there are human creations. Recognition of the human authorship of any view of death is the first step away from nature as an alleged source of independent meaning and the first step toward an alternative, more human meaning of "natural" death.

That alternative is the opposite of the first three meanings. It is the view that the natural is not a referent outside human experience but, on the contrary, is that which is most essentially human. The death that is natural is a human creation. Moreover, because the most fundamental character of human existence is the uniqueness of the individual, the natural can only be a personal creation. Death is determined *by the individual* to be natural when it is informed with a meaning and accomplished in a manner congruent with that person's uniqueness: it becomes most natural when it is a crafted artifice, a deliberate endeavor not to perish simply as a mutable part of the natural order. Because the essence of human experience is the personal, not the general, the meaning of natural death cannot be framed in general terms, such as peaceful death, dying without apparatus, or death after ninety. Natural in human terms can be defined only by the individual.

Is there a special relationship between aging and this meaning of natural death? Using the individual concept of natural, is it possible to consider death more natural in old age than in earlier years? Keeping in mind that natural here means not artless but its opposite, the styling of a highly personal creation, the answer is yes. That answer has nothing to do with old age viewed as a good time to die. It has to do only with the likelihood that the older a person becomes, the more practiced he or she becomes in that most engaging of human projects—the elaborating of one's own unique-ness. Older persons may be more able than younger ones to create for themselves a death that is natural, in the same way that experienced artists are able to create works of art with greater ease than are beginning artists. This does not mean that with increasing ability to fashion a death of one's own, there necessarily comes an increasing acceptance of death. On the contrary, the more accomplished a person becomes in expressing unique-ness, the more absurd death may seem as an annihilation of the irreplace-able individual. Thus the view of death that an individual fashions as personally natural may be one in which life has inestimable value and death is despised.

Ethical issues in the care of dying elderly, as in terminal care generally, derive from the particular view of death that an individual patient holds.[9] Since there is no intrinsic connection between age and a person's subjective measure of "long enough," there are no grounds for expecting older patients to hold a particular view or acceptance of death that would distinguish them from other patients. The serious danger, however, is that when elderly persons are vulnerable, they will accept from their social and medical milieu an external view of the naturalness of their death. The moral responsibility of their caregivers thus is twofold. Not only have health professionals the duty to provide treatment measures strictly in keeping with the individual patient's own view of death. In addition, they bear the still greater responsibility to assist patients in asserting their uniqueness in the face of social expectations, that is, the responsibility to assist them in the fashioning of their personal understanding of death's meaning for them.

Because there is no external criterion whereby one could judge for a patient that death is natural in the subjective sense, it follows that no one can provide for another a natural death. Thus, when an elderly patient's views cannot be ascertained, there is no justification for deciding on the basis of age that the life has been long enough. Death may be allowed by proxy decision based on other considerations, such as the degree of suffering imposed upon the person by being kept alive, but age cannot be a factor in deciding that the life has come to a natural close. The natural relationship between death and aging is that which an elderly person determines individually. For that decision there can be no proxy.

Notes

1. A. Chekhov, "Misery," in *Great Stories by Chekhov* (New York: Dell, 1976).
2. R. A. Burt, "Legal Reform and Aging: Current Issues, Troubling Trends," in *What Does it Mean to Grow Old?*, ed. T. R. Cole and S. A. Gadow (Durham, N.C.: Duke University Press, 1986).
3. R. Blythe, *The View in Winter, Reflections on Old Age* (New York: Penguin Books, 1980).
4. Ibid.
5. L. Thomas, "Death in the Open," *New England Journal of Medicine* (11 January 1973): 92-3.
6. H. T. Engelhardt, *Foundations of Bioethics* (New York: Oxford University Press, 1986).
7. K. Woodward, "Instant Repulsion: Decrepitude, the Mirror Stage, and the Literary Imagination," *The Kenyon Review* (Fall 1983): 43-66.
8. A. C. MacIntyre, *After Virtue: A Study in Moral Theory* (Notre Dame, Ind.: University of Notre Dame Press, 1981).
9. S. A. Gadow, "Caring for the Dying: Advocacy or Paternalism," *Death Education* 3 (1980): 387-98.

In Whose Image?
Ethical Issues in Genetic Engineering
Thomas H. Murray

"Genetic engineering" is a suitably evocative name for the large set of activities having in common only their fundamental method: the systematic rearrangement of genetic material. It is quite literally a form of engineering—only rather than bridges, girders, dams, or the like, what is being manipulated is nothing less than the raw material of heredity, deoxyribosenucleic acid—DNA—and what is being fabricated is precisely new forms of life. As a technology, it has generated in roughly equal measures grand hopes and terrifying fears: everything from cancer-gobbling cells to Andromeda strains or, as one journalistic wag suggested, a flying nun.

While it is not true, as some cynics suppose, that technology was invented to provide employment for moral philosophers, it is certainly true that technologies, including genetic engineering, often raise ethical questions. This idea, usually stated crudely along the lines that "technology creates moral problems," has attained the status of an aphorism. Like many an aphorism, though, this one holds an important truth. We can state its truth roughly this way: where there is no human choice, there can be no moral dilemma, since there can be no possibility of human action making any difference. I cannot be held morally responsible for things over which I have no control, not even indirect control. Technologies create possibilities for human action and control where they did not exist before. Once we have the means of intervening, we face the choice whether or not to do so. To the extent that the choices we face affect the fates of persons—and few choices fail that test—they are, at least in part, *moral* choices. And when the moral superiority of one option over all others is not clear, we may confront a moral dilemma.

Looking at the relation of technology and moral problems in this way usefully reminds us of two truths. First, and more often stated in criticisms of technology, is the fact that decisions whether and how to adopt technologies are just that—decisions. While the spread of a technology may seem to be carried by a momentum of its own, that is an illusion attributable to the phenomena of multiple decision makers each choosing in isolation from other deciders. As decisions, they may and often ought to include consideration of the ethical dimensions of the choice, both of individual choices and of the aggregate of choices.

The second truth, a part of which is commonly emphasized by proponents of the technology, begins by noting that the power technology grants us may be used for human good. Take an example familiar to anyone who has seen a modern medical intensive care unit: the mechanical ventilator. The ventilator was created to aid people whose lungs could not function well enough to get sufficient oxygen to their tissues and organs. It was intended as a stopgap—a device that could tide a person over a crisis, until their lungs recovered and the ventilator could be removed. A marvelous, lifesaving technology. Unfortunately, not all people who were placed on mechanical ventilators regained the use of their lungs. Some simply died anyway: a sadness, perhaps in part a tragedy; but *not* a moral dilemma. Others hung on, but could not be weaned from the ventilator. (Yes, "weaned" is exactly the word used, with all its connotations of infantile dependence on the one hand and life-giving nurturance and caring on the other.) To thoughtful physicians, nurses, patients, and families, the question would arise, Is the light worth the candle? Is the person for whose diaphragmatic muscles the ventilator was substituting really benefitting from it? The answer quite often was, Yes; but other times the answer was, possibly, probably, or almost certainly, No. What then should we do? Disconnect the ventilator? Thus comes the now-familiar phrase "pulling the plug." Technology gave us a choice where before we had none. Sometimes the choice was obvious, and a great deal of good came from the technology. But at other times the choice was a profoundly difficult one, and we were forced to struggle with a moral dilemma. Yes, technology created a dilemma. But in the case of the mechanical ventilator, as with most technologies that are adopted, it was the prospect of serving human good or at least the interests of particular persons that led us to accept the technology in the first place. And the dilemmas it creates are the thin advancing edge of an effort that trails much good in its wake. So, when we say that "technology creates moral dilemmas," we should not lose sight of the good that the same technology may also do. We should not, that is, abandon a technology because it occasionally thrusts us into ethical dilemmas.

One of the great difficulties we encounter when trying to understand the impact of a new technology is our faint ability to anticipate its long-term effects. Just what changes a complex, multi-faceted technology such as genetic engineering will engender is impossible to predict. Oh, we may offer educated guesses about the impact in any one area—say on efficiency in the manufacture of pharmaceuticals. But perhaps more important will be subtle changes in areas we do not even anticipate. For example, it seems likely that over time our attitude towards living things of all kinds, including human life, will alter as purposive engineering of those forms of life becomes commonplace.

Genetic engineering could have as profound an impact on the way we think about humankind's place and significance in the universe as did other revolutionizing ideas. Galileo's and Copernicus's evidence that the earth revolved around the sun displaced our idea that the earth, and its inhabitants, was literally at the center of the universe. Darwin's and Wallace's theory of natural evolution showed that the complexity of life was imaginable without purposive creation, and that humans and animals shared common ancestral roots. And Freud revealed the depths of irrationality that could move us to action and, more frightening, afflict our most prized capacity, our reason. As we learn more about the genetic determinants of animal and human traits, and as we acquire increasing abilities to alter genetic makeup and thereby modify traits, it seems more likely than not that we will come to think differently about ourselves. "Differently" in this case need not mean "worse," but it almost certainly will mean some troubled times as we try to reinterpret the grounds for our belief in the significance— dare we say sacredness?—of humankind. Neither Galileo nor Darwin nor Freud shattered our belief in our own dignity and significance, even as they threatened, and continue to threaten, some of the ways people have understood the source of that significance. There is no reason to think that genetic engineering will do finally what other scientific revolutions have failed to do. This is not, by the way, a plea for "secular humanism," whatever that may be. Sophisticated religious traditions have successfully come to terms with each of the transformational ideas already mentioned, and there is little doubt that they will be able to do the same with genetic engineering. Certainly, scholars in those traditions have been some of our best guides through the moral complexities of genetic engineering.

Technologies affect cultures in at least two ways. On the one hand, they transform practices—what we do and the way we do it. These changes in practices can, with time, affect the way we come to think about a number of things, not least of which is the significance of our own existence. Less commonly, technologies, scientific discoveries, or other ideas can more directly transform the way we think about ourselves. Genetic engineering has the power to do both.

The many worries that have been voiced about genetic engineering have as their core two distinct sources of anxiety: nature's inscrutability, or humankind's fallibility. The concern expressed about, for example, what might happen if genetically engineered bacteria are released over a strawberry field reflects principally the conviction that we do not know enough about nature, specifically about ecology, to be assured that no catastrophic consequences will follow. The inscrutability of nature may not permit us to know with any confidence that the risks of such a release are containable and acceptable. How can we address this worry? We can use science to learn more about nature, and to a degree at least dispel some of the uncertainty. We can, that is, make nature a little less inscrutable.

Our concern with humankind's fallibility is more difficult to address. People are often unwise and sometimes untrustworthy. Especially in situations where individuals may be influenced by their pride of creation or by their financial interests, we are prudent to ask if their judgments are genuinely sound. A scientist who has spent years developing a modified microbe, or whose firm's future survival rests upon a speedy and successful field test of such a bug has many reasons to believe that the risk of such a test is small or nonexistent, only a few of which depend on scientific data. We know this, and we know we must be cautious about relying on a narrow decision-making process dominated by people whose interests are tied closely to particular outcomes.

One other aspect of decisions about what to pursue in genetic engineering deserves mention. Our fears about human fallibility are ameliorated when decisions are made deliberatively and openly. Those same fears are heightened however when decisions are reached in secret and carried out surreptitiously. Secrecy, then, is an especially significant source of concern within genetic engineering.

The list of ethical issues raised by genetic engineering is long and ungainly. It may be helpful to think of them as falling into three broad categories. First are concerns about the consequences of genetic engineering for the health of the public and the integrity of the environment. Among the issues in this category are the specters of Andromeda-like epidemics, and the accidental or deliberate release of modified microorganisms into the environment. We could call this category transforming our health and environment.

A second set of issues concerns possible transformations of our institutions. Most of the worries focus on the changes wrought within universities and within the scientific profession by the prospect of sudden and great wealth lurking just beyond the next petri dish. I am unaware of anything remotely approaching the recent and continuing conversion of large numbers of biological scientists into commercial entrepreneurs. The tensions this has created within academic institutions and within the community of scientists are many and severe.

The third set of issues concern nothing less than the transformation of humankind. While most people have heard of human gene therapy in this context, there are other, possibly more substantial transformations being made possible by genetic engineering as we acquire the ability to produce commercially and use those substances that regulate our own growth, development, and function.

Transforming Our Health and Environment

Genetic engineering holds great promise for the improvement of human health, as new drugs that better emulate the action of their naturally-occurring analogues, and more effective, highly-targeted systems for delivering such drugs become available. But the possibility that human health could be adversely affected was one of the chief sources of opposition to (and caution in) genetic engineering research. At first, there was much talk about a so-called "andromeda strain," a super-infectious and super-lethal new microorganism. (Indeed, it is occasionally suggested by those with a fearful and suspicious bent that the Human Immunodeficiency Virus—the virus that causes AIDS—was created by genetic engineering, despite the complete lack of evidence for the belief, including new evidence that the virus was present much earlier than previously supposed.) Concern to prevent the creation or release of such microbes led to the creation of sophisticated "containment" systems, physical and biological. Physical containment was set at four different levels, with the highest-dubbed "P-4"—the only one suitable for handling especially dangerous organisms. Biological containment was accomplished by developing organisms that could survive only under extraordinary conditions, likely to be found only in a laboratory. This could be done by, for example, using bacteria that needed a highly specific chemical to survive that could not be found in sufficient concentration outside of a special growth medium. These containment mechanisms, along with accumulated experience of dealing with genetically engineered organisms, have calmed most such fears. But human fallibility and judgment have resurrected those fears on occasion. In the summer of 1984, a junior official in the Pentagon asked for a routine reallocation of funds for a number of minor projects including an "aerosol test facility" in Utah. The procedure was a routine way of handling budget-year-end juggling for uncontroversial projects. The "aerosol test facility," it turned out, was a P-4 lab for research on biological warfare. At the time, only four P-4 labs existed in the entire country. The Army insisted that it intended to do only defensive research, although some scientists claimed that much of the appropriate research could be done with less pathogenic agents, under much less stringent conditions.[1] The apparently surreptitious manner in which the Army attempted to get approval from Congress for funding the proposed laboratory, and its express purpose for research on biological warfare, do little to assure the critics of genetic engineering.

Another arena for biotechnology is agriculture. New crop strains could be developed by methods much more direct and efficient than the previous tools we had for inducing and selecting variants. Biotechnology could also conceivably contribute to agriculture by developing microorganism variants that would help farmers. If, for example, we could create a benign microbe that replaced another one that caused crop damage, we could increase yield.[2] Among the first to be developed was a variant of *pseudomonas syringae*, a bacteria that acts as a nucleus for the formation of ice crystals in plants. The new bug does not promote ice formation. If it would displace its ice-loving cousin in a potato field, for example, the plants could withstand a modest frost and thus the growing season could be expanded. To be successful, though, we would have to release the new bacteria over open fields. The initial proposals to do field tests of "ice-minus" (as the modified *P. syringae* was nicknamed) were fiercely opposed.[3] Part of the opposition was based on the claim that none of the people involved in approving the study had the necessary expertise in ecology. This form of ignorance can be remedied by consulting with experts in ecology, and this is what was done.

Transforming Our Institutions

Money is a powerful force in most institutions, as well as for most individuals. Universities and scientists are no exceptions. Changes in modern university-based science have combined with the emerging, fiercely entrepreneurial biotechnology industry, some characteristics of recombinant DNA research, and old-fashioned greed to create a potent mixture that may threaten two closely linked institutions—science and the university.

While it may have been possible a few decades ago to fund scientific research out of one's back pocket, the increasing sophistication and cost of scientific equipment have made modern science into a heavily capital-intensive enterprise. Paying the researcher's salary, buying a few test tubes and chemicals is no longer enough. Now we must outfit sometimes huge laboratories with awcsomely complex—and expensive—instruments, computers, and the like. Donald Kennedy, the president of Stanford University, argues that we entered the era of what he dubs "Big Science" when "[t]he capital cost of the equipment and special facilities . . . had become larger than the capital value of the endowment necessary to yield the faculty member's salary."[4] Research universities have a perpetual need to find the money necessary to support first-rate research.

People with money usually want to make more. So they look for investments. Perhaps the hottest investment opportunities in the early 1980s were the new biotechnology companies. By mid-1985, investment in the biotechnology industry topped 2.5 *billion* dollars—almost 850 million dollars in 1983 alone. (Investor interest has cooled somewhat since then.[5]) We had then, and continue to have, a number of companies, many of them small, with virtually no products to sell, but with enormous sums of money to spend on research and development.

The line between applied research and basic research may be drawn a number of different ways and with greater or lesser confidence. One way to think about the distinction is to conceive of *basic* research as pursuing questions because of their fundamental scientific significance, while *applied* research takes its questions from other quarters—for example, industry's desire for profitable products. Rarely has the line been so narrow as it is in genetic engineering where today's "basic" research suggests almost immediately tomorrow's application. [One caveat here: applied research is not product development. Applied scientific research may be necessary to develop a new, marketable product, but there will be a long wait and many intervening steps between even applied research and commercial application.] University-based scientists who are highly skilled at basic research may also, in the case of genetic engineering, find themselves suddenly and remarkably useful to the biotechnology industry.

Scientists are human, even scientists who work in universities. They have need of money for themselves, and to support their research. Especially at the major research universities, scientists are expected to raise, through grants and contracts, a good deal of the money necessary to support their research, often including a portion of their own salaries. While much of this support comes from one or another federal agency such as the National Institutes of Health, the National Science Foundation, or the Department of Energy, there are other sources as well including charitable foundations and industry. For academic scientists in genetic engineering, a relationship with the biotechnology industry is particularly common. While industry supports approximately 3 to 4 percent of all research in higher education institutions, according to one study it supports 16 to 24 percent of biotechnology research in the same institutions—to the tune of roughly 120 million dollars.[6] The same study estimates that 46 percent of all biotechnology firms provide funds for university research. For some companies, university research is a major part of their research and development investment: about one in five spends over 20 percent of its R&D dollars on university research. For the biotech firms, it appears to be a good investment. Per dollar spent, university-based research yields over four times as many patent applications as research done within the company.

With such a neat complementarity of needs and capabilities between the biotechnology industry and academic scientists, why should we worry? In fact, there are concerns about the effects of this powerful combination of needs, interests, and money on two institutions—the university and science.

We should not romanticize the university, where political battles—especially over resources and prestige—can be as bitter as in any organization. But at the same time, universities are different from profit-seeking organizations. Among the goals of the university is the mission to create and transmit knowledge *for its own sake*, and not because the particular knowledge serves any crass utilitarian purpose. In order to accomplish this mission, universities must sustain a delicate balance between various disciplines, some of whom may be momentarily flush while others are impoverished. They must assure the intellectual independence of researchers and students, even while accepting money from an assortment of people and organizations with interests and agendas of their own. Balance and independence are difficult to maintain when large infusions of money—always necessary to the continuing vitality of the institution—tend to throw things out of kilter.

Power follows money in universities as in other institutions. Faculty who get large research grants or contracts become powerful within their departments; departments that swell with research monies become powerful within their universities. If there is money in doing applied research for biotechnology companies, scientists will be inclined to turn their endeavors in that direction, and away from basic research; the power within the department may swing then towards applied researchers. A department awash with research funds will be inclined to swing its weight within the university, tipping the balance of power towards their own department and away from less commercializable disciplines.

The more dependent universities become on industry support, the more dangerous it becomes to offend those supporters. One fear is that financial dependence will lead to intellectual timidity. There are more direct threats to the university's independence. Thirty-two percent of biotech firms support the training of graduate and post-doctoral students. A third of those firms place some *quid pro quo* on their support, stipulating the sort of research the student must do, or requiring that the person work for the firm now or later.

Science too is threatened. While the competitive world of industry thrives on secrecy, the equally competitive world of science thrives on openness. Scientists keep secrets, but not for long, because success in science is measured by publication of new discoveries. The important thing is to publish first. Typically, scientists have also been willing to share techniques and materials, as well as preliminary reports of findings. Industry sponsorship of academic researchers has changed that. Companies derive no benefit from research if the results are shared freely and widely. They prefer to develop patents or trade secrets. In addition to the large number of patent applications stemming from industry-sponsored university research in biotechnology, 41 percent of the biotech companies investing in university research have derived at least one trade secret from their investment. This suggests that a strong current of secrecy has swept into the historically open university laboratory. Unless this is contained, it threatens to distort science and seriously disrupt progress in basic research.

Transforming Ourselves

Genetic engineering may allow us to transform ourselves in at least three ways. First, we may directly alter our genetic makeup through what is usually called gene therapy. Second, we may use the products of genetic engineering such as hormones to modify our physiology and even our anatomy. Third, we may transform the way we think of ourselves.

On June 20, 1980, the General Secretaries of the National Council of Churches, the Synagogue Council of America, and the United States Catholic Conference sent a letter to the President of the United States. In that letter they warned of several dangers posed by genetic engineering. About the modification of man, they wrote: "History has shown us that there will always be those who believe it appropriate to 'correct' our mental and social structures by genetic means, so as to fit their vision of humanity. This becomes more dangerous when the basic tools to do so are finally at hand. Those who would play God will be tempted as never before."[7]

The General Secretaries' historical observation is accurate. There have been numerous attempts to "correct" human characteristics, usually by controlling reproduction. Those judged genetically inferior were sterilized or discouraged from having offspring. Those thought to be genetically superior were encouraged to mate and have many children. The most infamous such program was undertaken in Nazi Germany. But there have been eugenic movements in many countries, including the United States. While these programs were based on fallacious pseudo-science and were generally ineffective, they managed to harm many persons. Contemporary genetic engineering provides a much better understanding of human genetics and the prospect of more precise control. It does not, unfortunately, provide us with any greater wisdom that would permit us to know what sorts of human characteristics are genuine "improvements" and what characteristics are merely out of fashion for a time, or within a particular subculture.

Deciding which human traits are desirable and which are undesirable is not a scientific question; rather, it is a moral, social, and political one. For the most part, we are better off not enforcing through genetic engineering any one particular view of what is desirable and undesirable. We must be extremely cautious not to fall into the same trap as our equally well-meaning forebears, who were convinced that their views were, naturally, correct.

But not all the potential uses of genetic engineering on humans are "eugenic" in the same sense. Not all are efforts aimed at the selection of what one or another group regards as desirable traits. The most likely uses of direct genetic manipulation will be to correct what everyone agrees are terrible diseases that have a relatively simple and direct genetic cause. There are a number of diseases that appear to be caused by a single abnormal gene. Many of them are lethal, some at a very early age. Others, by an evolutionary quirk, do not afflict people until middle age or later. Huntington's disease, a degenerative disease of the nervous system, is caused by a single gene. The gene is dominant: it will be expressed even though the person has a paired normal gene. Because an individual has already had an opportunity to reproduce—and pass the gene along to offspring—the gene for Huntington's, unlike other dominant lethal genes, does not tend to extinguish itself. If there were a way to replace or alter the expression of the Huntington's gene, people could be spared the great suffering and early death that it now inflicts. Imagine that we now knew the precise gene that causes Huntington's (we are probably very close to that knowledge); that we were able to clone—reproduce precisely—the normal version of the same gene; that we had a way of introducing it into someone's body so that they would not suffer the ravages of the disease. There would be two very different strategies possible, corresponding to a distinction between two kinds of cells: germ cells, meaning those cells that are involved in reproduction—sperm, ova, and the undifferentiated cells that are their precursors; and somatic cells, meaning all others that will *not* be passed on to future generations.

Gene therapy on somatic cells is in essence similar to any other therapy that dies with the person without directly and intentionally altering his or her germ cells. While the person might live longer and healthier, and because of that be more likely to have children, it is no more true of somatic cell gene therapy than of any other conventional and familiar therapy such as insulin. Diabetics, who would suffer disease and death, would, as a consequence of insulin therapy, be much more likely to have children, just as would the person who benefitted from somatic cell gene therapy. In neither case would there have been any direct alteration of the genes of the children of these same individuals. For that to happen, germ cell gene therapy would have to be used.

In germ cell gene therapy, the intended effect is to alter the genetic composition of that individual and of all offspring who would inherit the altered gene. We do in fact alter people's germ cells in other ways: by radiation, natural and man-made; by a variety of chemicals in our environment or our diet. Even some therapies—both radiation therapy and chemotherapy—have the potential to alter a person's germ cells and thereby affect the genetic composition of offspring. In contrast to germ cell therapy, though, these other therapies alter germ cells unintentionally and in an unsystematic, indeed unpredictable fashion. Germ cell therapy would attempt to make specific, intentional changes in genetic material.

At this time, research on germ cell gene therapy is banned. Somatic cell therapy, though, is permitted under very strict controls. Several research teams are working towards the goal of being the first to perfect a technique for such therapy, and for using it with human subjects. The early efforts are likely to be focused on lethal single-gene diseases for which the genes are well-known but for which no therapies are effective. Examples of such diseases are adenosine deaminase (ADA) deficiency, and Lesch-Nyhan disease, caused by an absence of the enzyme hypoxanthine-guanine phosphoribosyl transferase.[8] Some of the researchers working on somatic cell gene therapy have proven themselves to be exceptionally thoughtful about the ethics of such research. Paradoxically, this leads me to worry that the greatest ethical challenges posed by genetic engineering will come not from gene therapy, which is being closely watched, but from the large-scale commercial production of heretofore rare hormones and other regulatory substances, for example, human growth hormone.

Human growth hormone, or hGH, is a hormone that plays a crucial role in the complex system that controls growth of many body components including the long bones of the leg. Children who are deficient in hGH will be much shorter than normal—so short that the activities of everyday life that people of normal height take for granted become major obstacles. There are, in fact, a variety of conditions leading to short stature, of which hGH deficiency is only one, but a fairly common one. Many children and adolescents have benefitted from injections of hGH and have grown to normal or near-normal height.

Until recently, hGH was obtainable only from the pituitary glands of cadavers and was in chronically short supply. In 1985, a few recipients of hGH were found to suffer from Creutzfeld-Jakob Syndrome, a neurological disease caused by a so-called "slow" virus—a virus that takes a long time to manifest itself in its victims. It appears likely that in the preparation of cadaver hGH, at least one batch was contaminated with tissue that contained the Creutzfeld-Jakob virus. All cadaver hGH was pulled quickly from use. Fortunately, biotechnology companies came to the rescue with a human growth hormone produced by bacteria. Scientists had isolated the gene for hGH, inserted it into the bacteria, and coaxed the bug to produce quantities of the hormone adequate for commercial production.[9]

No longer limited by the natural scarcity of human pituitaries, hGH could now be produced in whatever quantities the market demanded. Here was the ethical problem: some people, believing that to be taller (within limits) was advantageous, sought to give that advantage to their children by procuring biosynthetic hGH for them. This phenomenon raises a number of difficult ethical issues: whether it is morally acceptable to use hGH to gain a social advantage rather than to treat a disease; whether children, who will be too young to consent, ought to be exposed to the pain of such treatment without a reason related to health; whether the expensive treatment would result in the wealthy buying yet one more advantage for their children; and whether the proper response to a form of unwarranted social discrimination—"heightism," it has been called—is to look for a technological "fix" rather than to address the social roots of the problem. Would we seriously consider, for example, countering racism by making everyone the same color? If not, then why not deal with heightism by reaffirming that people's dignity, talent, and worth do not depend, except in extremely limited circumstances, on height.

The challenge posed by biosynthetic hGH is just one of the first of many such problems likely to come our way along with the great good that can also come from genetic engineering.

Notes

1. R. Jeffrey Smith, "New Army Biowarfare Lab Raises Concerns," *Science* 226 (7 December 1984): 1176-78.
2. Winston J. Brill, "Safety Concerns and Genetic Engineering in Agriculture," *Science* 227 (25 January 1985): 381-84.
3. Colin Norman, "Judge Halts Gene-splicing Experiment," *Science* 224 (1 June 1984): 962-63.
4. Donald Kennedy, "Government Policies and the Cost of Doing Research," *Science* 227 (1 February 1985): 480-84.
5. Mark Crawford, "Biotech Market Changing Rapidly," *Science* 231 (3 January 1986): 12-14.
6. David Blumenthal et al., "Industry Support of University Research in Biotechnology," *Science* 231 (17 January 1986): 242-46.
7. "Letter from Three General Secretaries," reprinted as appendix B in President's Commission for the Study of Ethical Problems in Medicine and Biomedical and Behavioral Research, *Splicing Life* (Washington, D.C.: U.S. Government Printing Office, 1982).
8. W. French Anderson, "Prospects for Human Gene Therapy," *Science* 226 (26 October 1984): 401-409.
9. Gina Kolata, "New Growth Industry in Human Growth Hormone?" *Science* 234 (3 October 1986): 22-24.

A Glimpse at Galveston's
Medical Past, 1836-1885

Chester R. Burns

When humans experience diarrhea, vomiting, fever, and other pains and miseries of illness, they usually respond in three ways. They try to explain the causes of the changes that are called diseases, they use drugs, perform operations, and employ other methods to eliminate the symptoms and miseries, and they try to discover ways to prevent the diseases from recurring. Between 1836 and 1885, Galvestonians exhibited all three patterns of response to their experiences with illness.

Diseases

In the beginning, Galveston was a "rough village," with a few frame houses, a few sheds for waterfront storage, and some grass huts that housed Mexican prisoners.[1] The Congress of the Republic of Texas made Galveston a port of entry, and Gail Borden, Jr., became Collector of Customs for the port in June of 1837. In October of that year, a hurricane devastated the island, leaving only one structure still standing. Rebuilding was rapid. In May of 1838, the Congress of the Republic of Texas journeyed from Houston to Galveston on the steamboat Friendship. They were impressed with the enthusiasm and hospitality of the growing number of Galvestonians who had arrived in the city during the early months of 1838. A few weeks later, the county of Galveston was established as a political entity.

During the spring and summer of 1838, numerous structures were built on the east end of the island.[2] The Strand was a popular site; new buildings included a customs house, some private homes, a hotel, some warehouses and commercial stores, and a saloon and restaurant at the corner of 23rd and Strand. The buildings on the north side of the Strand were built over a quagmire of marshy water and filth that existed between the bay and the higher, drier land on the south side of the Strand. In January of 1839, the 300 or so townspeople of Galveston incorporated as a city.

There was a steady influx of new residents; some think that more than a thousand persons resided in the city by late September when the first major epidemic of yellow fever began.[3] By December of 1839, when the epidemic had abated, there were only about 600 persons living in Galveston. How many died and how many moved away is not known exactly. The appearance of yellow fever was terrifying. A twenty-five-year-old man would be healthy one day and dead three days later, having passed steadily from debility, fever, and pains in the extremities and loins, to a stage of vomiting blood clots (called the "black vomit"), to jaundice and death.

What could cause such a miserable death? There was a strong belief in a causal relationship between weather and disease. Some thought that electricity in the atmosphere predisposed to yellow fever; thus epidemics in Galveston were explained by the frequent lightning and thunderstorms in the area. Changes from hot to cool or dry to humid were also thought to be important.

Some believed that yellow fever could only be imported onto the island by those who were already sick. Reports about the presence or absence of yellow fever in New Orleans were inserted in the Galveston newspapers with obsessive regularity, because Galvestonians fully expected an epidemic when one existed in New Orleans. When the epidemic form of yellow fever did arrive, it was believed to spread "through contagion, encouraged by uncleanness and noxious gases."[4] These believers in contagion advocated quarantines that disrupted business and trade. Moreover, strict contagionists had no quarrel with anyone who wanted to flee from an epidemic.

Others did not believe in importation or contagion. They thought that substances emanating from reservoirs of filth could cause yellow fever. Such miasmata were associated with the noxious gases and vapors that arose from pools of stagnant water and piles of decaying garbage that dotted the city's landscape. Believing in the local origin of yellow fever, such anti-contagionists were strong advocates of sanitary cleanups and elimination of smelly marshes and garbage heaps.

In July of 1839, Ashbel Smith had journeyed to Galveston for some days of rest and relaxation. A graduate of Yale Medical School, Smith had recently resigned after two years as Surgeon General of the Army of the Republic of Texas. During the epidemic of yellow fever that started in late September, Smith did not get much rest. While treating many patients, he was impressed with the fact that all of the cases occurred in individuals who lived on the Strand, and that no one living in other parts of the island acquired the disease, even though they had had contact with some of the afflicted.[5] Thus, Smith concluded that the disease was not contagious, and confirmed this for himself by tasting the "black vomit" from patients, more than once. But, he did believe that there was an association between the disease and the marshy, filthy waters underneath the Strand's buildings, and he also believed that the disease would abate after the first frost, which it did in early November.

There were only about 600 persons living in Galveston by December of 1839.[6] How many died and how many moved away is not known exactly.

Yellow fever epidemics occurred on the island again in 1844, 1847, 1853, 1854, 1858, 1859, 1864, and 1867.[7] During the epidemic of 1847, Smith himself almost died from the disease. Given this frequency, it is not surprising that Galvestonians feared yellow fever more than any other disease.

In the absence of epidemic yellow fever, a typical mortality report would read like the one for the two weeks between July 1 and July 16, 1859:

> Wm Fisher, 3 mo., diarrhea
> Negro child of Gen. Green, 4 mo., diarrhea
> Annie Diebour, 2 years, whooping cough
> Robt. Crawford, 9 mo., teething
> J.W. Ruble, 3 mo., diarrhea
> Wm. McCoy, 40 years, consumption
> Carl Buggs, 58 years, dysentery
> Chas. Bohling, 9 mo., consumption
> Mrs. Sophia Wernn, 22 years, diarrhea
> Christian Ratoff, 8 mo., diarrhea
> Chas. C. Phillips, 10 mo., teething
> Negro woman, 75 years, old age
> H.A.F. Beverkohne, 6 weeks, convulsion[8]

Note that nine of these thirteen deaths were under the age of two years. Mortality among infants and children was very high. In 1866, for example, there were 477 recorded deaths in Galveston.[9] Forty percent were under the age of ten years; seventy-five percent were under the age of forty years. Most of the labels used for the diseases in this mortality report suggest some infectious process, such as cholera or typhoid fever.

But these were not the only causes of mortality and morbidity during the first fifty years of Galveston's existence. Twenty-eight persons died of drowning in 1866; this was a recurrent hazard in an island environment. Accidents also occurred. In February of 1859, Rev. Benjamin Eaton received a serious thigh wound from an encounter with a supposedly tame deer in a wooded area next to the church he served.[10] In May of 1859, Stephen Kirkland died after a fall from the piazza of an upper story at his house.[11] There were boat accidents rather often, resulting in injuries that sometimes required amputations of limbs.

Some infants were stillborn; a few people died of old age. Some died of cancer, consumption, dropsy of the heart, sunstroke, or gunshot wounds. For the Civil War years of 1861-1865, lists of Texans wounded in battle were published regularly.[12] Early in the war, these lists indicated slightly, severely, or mortally wounded. Later, the wounded parts were named. Some Galvestonians also died of "whiskey exposure," "bad whiskey," or "entemperance."[13] In January of 1872, a fourteen-year-old boy was run over by a streetcar.

By the 1870s, though, Galveston was heralded as the "healthiest seaport in the world."[14] Some also believed that the death rate in Galveston was less than any other city in the United States. Local newspapers reported often that "The city is remarkably healthy." Even with the fear of yellow fever, Galveston was thought to be a healthy place to live or visit. After all, as early as 1839, Ashbel Smith had come to Galveston to recuperate from overwork and illness experienced in Houston.

Pills and Practices

Physicians who treated yellow fever victims in Galveston believed that their remedies made a difference in the outcome. Their experiences and their statistics could not be denied.

In 1839, Ashbel Smith had treated a thirty-year-old man with yellow fever.[15] Upon seeing him for the first time, Smith promptly took enough blood from the patient to cause fainting. He covered the patient carefully and placed his feet in a warm mustard bath, all of which produced "copious perspiration." He prescribed a cathartic, a "senna and rhubarb infusion," which emptied his bowels. Within two days, the patient was convalescent; two days later, he resumed his usual activities. The man had been very sick and he sought medical help immediately. Said Smith, ". . . in no one was there greater promptness in demanding the resources of the healing art." Now, he was well. How could anyone deny that "the resources of the healing art" had made the difference?

And so it went throughout this period, even though there was variation in the treatments given by physicians. Smith altered his approaches as he gained more experience during the epidemic of 1839. He was a careful observer, and he evaluated his therapeutic protocols most critically. When the disease was attacked very early, he believed that it was "very easily manageable."[16]

During the epidemic of 1858, physicians admitted 130 yellow fever victims to Galveston's city hospital.[17] No more than ten of these died. Local citizens believed that the disease yielded "readily to medical treatment."[18]

But a sick person did not have to seek a physician to obtain treatment. At least three treatment regimens were published in the *Galveston Weekly News* during this epidemic.[19] One was offered by a physician in Houston. Each could be handled by anyone who had the recommended ingredients— castor oil, oil of peppermint, molasses, castile soap, salt, mustard, quinine, orange tea, water, or blankets. In all of these, perspiration and purging were the main objectives. Bloodletting was not included, exemplifying a major change occurring in medical treatment throughout the country.

Some physicians though, were reluctant to discard bloodletting. Dr. Thomas Stanwood of Galveston thought that this practice was sadly neglected. With democratic fervor, he had proclaimed in 1855, "In a country like ours, every man, and especially every head of a family, should be able to use the lancet, and a case of lancets, in good order, should be considered as indispensable a part of furniture for housekeeping, as knives and forks, or any culinary or other utensils."[20] Stanwood also believed in the use of calomel and other mercurial preparations for purging,[21] and in the use of opiates for calming the body's overall response to harmful stimuli.[22]

Opiates were among the secret ingredients in several of the proprietary medicines that had become so popular by mid-century. If Galvestonians of that era had not wanted to be treated by a regular physician, they could have selected any one of a remarkable variety of medicinal mixtures.

For example, nine different ads appeared in the February 19, 1861, issue of the *Galveston Weekly News*. A sick Galvestonian then could have chosen Hostetter's Stomach Bitters; or Dr. Leroy's French Specific for All Affections of the Urinary Organs, and these Affections Only; or Winer's Canadian Vermifuge; or Dr. J. Bovee Dods' Imperial Wine Bitters; or Daly's Aromatic Valley Whiskey for Medicinal Purposes; or Brown's Bronchial Troches; or Sanford's Liver Invigorator; or Sanford's Family Blood Purifying Pills; or Old Sachem Bitters and Wigwam Tonic. Using the names of foreign countries was popular. Everyone knew that Redding's Russia Salve Vegetable Ointment cured more than 40 diseases because it was Russianized, or that Mexican Mustang Liniment was surely good for Texans if it was good for Mexican mustangs.

A Prof. Holloway believed that he had a moral duty to advertise his medicines; after all, he had been rewarded with "fortune, fame, and the gratitude of millions."[23] Such was the ethic; such was the hope of the vendors of proprietary medicines during this era. Galvestonians helped to sustain that hope. Almost every issue of most newspapers published in Galveston contained advertisements for these medicines. Several ads reappeared year after year, suggesting that public consumption continued year after year.

After general anesthetics began to be used more extensively during the 1850s, Galvestonians permitted more surgical operations. Experiences during the Civil War had been most instructive for surgeons. During the 1860s and 1870s, Galveston's doctors performed operations for such conditions as umbilical, scrotal, and inquinal hernias; urethral strictures; broken or infected bones; vesico-vaginal fistulas; and bladder stones.[24] They reported successful outcomes.

Preventives

Many of the proprietary or patent medicines were advertised as preventives. Galvestonians surely swallowed these medicines with hopes they would prevent future pain and suffering, especially that from yellow fever.

A New Orleans physician had provided the working men of that city with a regimen "guaranteed" to prevent yellow fever. In early September of 1858, the editor of the *Galveston Weekly News* reprinted these exhortations:

"I. Take no food for two days, and only drink ice water, river in preference to rain water.

II. Eat flesh meat for the next two days; but use no fat, no bread, no vegetables.

III. Keep from labor for one week. When you walk or sit, be sure to do so in the shade, or in the coolest place you can find."[25]

Whether any laborers in New Orleans or Galveston successfully negotiated for a week's vacation as a way to prevent yellow fever is not known. But, they probably liked the doctor's advice.

As mentioned earlier, those who believed that yellow fever was contagious thought that the disease could be prevented by quarantines. During the epidemic of 1839, a Board of Health established by the city council fired the Post and City Physician for insolence, incompetency, and failure to enforce quarantine regulations.[26] Subsequently, these regulations were enforced although the Houston *Telegraph* condemned them as inconvenient from a commercial point of view.[27] Moreover, everyone knew that quarantines had not halted the spread of yellow fever epidemics in Mobile, New Orleans, and Houston.

Neither did they in Galveston. Nevertheless, Galveston's city councils continued to adopt such regulations and continued to expect a local physician to enforce them. A quarantine station was constructed in 1853; others succeeded this one, in 1870, 1876, 1879, and 1885. Enforcement was fairly steady after 1870. During the quarantine season from May to November, 1884, for example, the physician assigned to the station in Galveston inspected 939 ships, and placed seventeen in twenty-day quarantines.[28]

Anti-contagionists, on the other hand, believed that there was a causal connection between the condition of a local environment and the incidence of yellow fever. One way to prevent future epidemics was to improve local conditions. In early June of 1857, the editor of the *Galveston Weekly News* exhorted citizens to "take every precaution to escape the epidemics which appear during the Summer." "Miasmic vapors, foul air, filth, intemperance" should be avoided. The city authorities should remove all nuisances. "Their olfactory organs should be awake night and day. A 'smelling committee' of the Common Council might be a useful institution just now. The villain who hid the dead cat in the sand on Tremont street, near our office, should be arrested, tried, and convicted of catocide, and sentenced to hunt up the fragments and carry them off. Ugh! shut the window—drown us with cologne!"[29]

Whether the cat was removed and the villain caught is not known. But, the city council did pass an ordinance requiring owners of buildings on the Strand to "fill up under their houses and raise the streets."[30] The Strand was raised some two to three feet, and many of the low places in the city were filled so that pools of stagnant water could not appear. These "sanitary movements" were hailed for giving the city a "clean and healthful appearance," and Galveston's oldest physicians (unnamed) declared that yellow fever could never become epidemic in Galveston again. That assertion was made in early August of 1858. During the two months following, an epidemic of yellow fever resulted in the deaths of at least 250 Galvestonians. Although perplexed and disillusioned by such experiences, the citizens of Galveston continued to support extensive sanitation efforts.

Medical Professionals

Some Galvestonians bought medicines from Dr. John Finn who had opened a drug store at the corner of 24th and Church during 1870. After retiring from thirty-seven years of medical practice, Finn knew which remedies really worked. His medicines were "guaranteed to cure permanently in from eight to fifteen days."[31] In September of 1875, he advertised that some 2,000 Galvestonians had already been cured with his medicines during the previous six months.

Some Galvestonians were treated by homeopathic doctors who were practicing in the city by the 1850s. Four or five were listed in the city directories of the 1870s and 1880s.

Many Galvestonians, though, supported the regular medical profession, whose members responded with heroic devotion. During the epidemic of 1858, for example, twenty-seven physicians provided medical care to yellow fever victims. Fourteen of these became sick with the disease; six of those died.[32] No one could claim that the physicians of Galveston fled from epidemics or avoided the seriously sick.

Galveston's citizens and governing authorities cooperated with physicians in efforts to solve health care problems. The earliest city councils authorized subcommittees of each council to act as hospital committees that actually functioned as local boards of health.[33] These committees inspected food markets, enforced quarantine regulations, and monitored activities at the city hospital.

The need for a place to house sick strangers was a problem from the very beginning of the city. A small frame building was provided during the earliest years; there may have been some rooms added, or a separate structure built during the early 1840s. The earliest city councils decided that funds were needed for the medical care of transients, poor citizens, and foreign seamen. They authorized the collection of a tax of one dollar for each passenger arriving from foreign ports. Captains of all ships were expected to present a list of their passengers and pay the fees. This money would be used to provide a hospital for the indigent and transient sick. By 1845, enough money had been collected to warrant construction of a new hospital building. Located at 9th and Strand, the new hospital was accepting patients by May of 1846. The building could accommodate about eighty-five patients, but it was usually overcrowded during epidemics of yellow fever.[34]

Both citizens and physicians were impressed with the low mortality of the yellow fever victims admitted to the hospital during the epidemic of 1858. Recall that only ten of 130 patients died. "This speaks well for the good management of that institution," said the editor of the *Galveston Weekly News*. Local doctors were astounded that some hospital patients with the black vomit even recovered. The mortality rate of patients admitted to the city hospital during years with no epidemics was also low. For example, in 1856, 275 patients were admitted and only sixteen died.[35] Altogether, Galvestonians were proud of their hospital, but concerned about the costs of operating it. "Should we patch our old hospital, or build a new brick one that would accommodate all patients...," asked one citizen in a letter dated December 28, 1858.[36] A new one was not built, and the old one deteriorated, especially during the Civil War years.

Although there were about 10,000 persons living in Galveston by the end of that war, the city had little money available for its hospital. Greensville Dowell leased the hospital from the city, and he was appointed city physician. He employed Dr. Charles Trueheart as an assistant. When the editor of the *Galveston Daily News* visited the hospital in late October of 1865, he was impressed with what had been accomplished by Dowell and Trueheart.[37] During that year, 190 patients had been admitted, of whom seven had died, 143 had been discharged, and forty remained. The wards were comfortable and clean; adequate medicines and food were provided.

Money for the care of these patients came from four sources. The city paid a fixed price for all patients sent by the mayor, usually those without homes or unable to pay. The county contributed for all insane persons and paupers. The U.S. government paid for the care of U.S. seamen. Others were considered to be private patients, with whites charged $2.00 per day, and blacks $1.50 per day.

Expenses for the county of Galveston for the year 1872 were published in a supplement to the *Galveston Daily News*.[38] The county had paid the Galveston Medical College Hospital $1,799.75 and St. Mary's Hospital $1,639.75. The county owed the city of Galveston $4,699.13 for care of county patients at the City Hospital. The city of Galveston also held bonds of the county amounting to over $11,000 for hospital expenses incurred during 1870 and 1871. County officials were quite alarmed about these costs for the care of the sick in Galveston's three hospitals.

The Galveston Medical College Hospital had not originated as a separate building. It was a section of the City Hospital that was leased to Greensville Dowell as the city physician and the dean of the medical college. Students participated in the care of patients admitted to the medical college's wards. By 1870, advertisements for the Galveston Medical College Hospital indicated that a separate structure adjacent to the college itself was used as a hospital for patients.

St. Mary's Infirmary, also called the Sisters of Charity Hospital, was built in 1867. The hospital advertised rooms with "ocean views and open-air rooftops."[39] By the end of 1869, the hospital had admitted 110 patients. Of these, ninety-six had been discharged, seven had died, and seven remained. Galvestonians were impressed with the quality of care given at what would soon be called St. Mary's Hospital.[40]

The expansion of hospital care was just one of several events signalling the professionalization of medicine on the island soon after the Civil War ended in April of 1865. The Galveston Medical Society adopted its constitution in July of 1865; the Galveston Medical College held its first classes in November of 1865; and the first issue of the *Galveston Medical Journal* was published in January of 1866.

On July 17, 1865, fourteen physicians adopted a constitution and by-laws establishing The Galveston Medical Society.[41] They also adopted the code of ethics of the American Medical Association. Within a year or so, there were twenty-five members. Although little is known about the activities of this group, it was surely an inspiration to other physicians in the state who created local societies during the Reconstruction Era. These local efforts culminated in the reorganization of the Texas State Medical Association, which held its first meeting in Houston on June 15, 1869.[42] Dr. T. J. Heard of Galveston was elected president. In 1877, the state society held its annual meeting on the island, and Dr. W.D. Kelly of Galveston served as president.[43]

The Galveston Medical College was known to most residents of the city as "Dowell's Medical College." The trustees of Soule University at Chappell Hill, the parent institution of the Galveston Medical College, appropriated $6,000 for a new medical college building that was built at 22nd and L streets in 1869. Greensville Dowell, dean of the school, actually lived in the building as caretaker.[44] Hence, the name: "Dowell's Medical College."

A student could be admitted to this college who possessed a "good intellect and a good moral constitution," was able to read and write, and could pay the required fees, which were, for example, $150 in 1866.[45] Room and board were available in private homes for $20 to $30 a month.

The annual term usually began in November and ended in March. Students attended lectures and visited patients in homes and on hospital wards. To graduate from the school, students had to complete all of the required courses, obtain certificates of good character from reputable physicians, and pass examinations in anatomy, chemistry, physiology, medicine, surgery, and obstetrics.[46] The first class had about two dozen students, three of whom graduated in the spring of 1866. For subsequent years, about thirty-five students matriculated each year, and about ten graduated each year.[47]

In the spring of 1868, some of the school's faculty members asked the trustees of Soule University to remove Dowell from the faculty. The trustees agreed, then reversed their decision, fearing that they had acted too hastily.[48] When most of the protesters resigned and left Galveston, the Galveston Medical College closed.

Dowell and several other doctors in Galveston then formed the Texas Medical College and Hospital.[49] This institution was chartered by the state. Sixty-eight-year-old Ashbel Smith served as president of the school's Board of Trustees, whose members represented all sections of the state. This board examined a number of professorial candidates during a three-month period before selecting seven to constitute the new faculty. This faculty decided to accept all students from the old Galveston Medical College, and they began courses in the fall of 1873. The school continued until 1881, when the faculty voluntarily ceased operations because they believed that the new state university would soon establish a medical school in Galveston.

Several of the physicians associated with the Galveston Medical College and with the Texas Medical College and Hospital were involved in efforts to create medical journals for the physicians of Texas.[50] The *Galveston Medical Journal* was the first medical journal published in Texas. Edited by Greensville Dowell, the first issue appeared in January of 1866. Dowell was worried about whether or not the 2,000 or so physicians in the state would support the journal. By December of 1866, there were nearly 600 subscribers.

Encouraged by this response and perhaps annoyed with the forceful Dowell, two of his colleagues at the medical college believed that the faculty as a group should publish a journal. They prepared two issues of what was to be called the *Texas Medical Journal*. They were printed in 1867, but not distributed because Dowell decided to purchase this new journal. Four issues of the new journal were published in 1868, but by May of that year, Dowell was the sole editor and only one journal, the *Galveston Medical Journal*, was being published. But, subscriptions waned, and the last issue was published in September of 1870.

In 1873, Dr. John D. Rankin of Galveston inaugurated a new journal titled *The Texas Medical Journal*.[51] This journal had an editorial board of six physicians. It was the state's only medical journal for six years. Lack of money again became a problem, and it ceased publication in 1879.

In January of 1881, a third journal appeared. It was named the *Texas Medical and Surgical Record*. Its editor was Dr. Cary H. Wilkinson, the physician-in-chief at St. Mary's Hospital. Although it was heralded as the official publication of the Texas State Medical Association, this new journal lasted only two years.

All of these efforts at professionalization, together with the continued patronage of sick citizens, encouraged more physicians to settle in Galveston. The population of the city was increasing too. Estimates for 1865, 1875, and 1885 were, respectively, 10,000, 20,000, and 25,000 persons. The number of regular physicians listed in the Galveston city directories for these years was, respectively, fifteen, fifty-two, and thirty-seven. In 1885, there were also eleven dentists, three midwives, five homeopathic physicians, and 173 saloons.

Conclusion

In this glimpse of health care in Galveston during the first fifty years of the city's existence, I have introduced some major themes that can be addressed by anyone attempting to reconstruct the city's medical past. There were few changes in the diseases and injuries afflicting Galveston's residents during these fifty years. Infectious diseases were the major cause of death. If they survived infancy and childhood, Galvestonians could expect to live to about the age that we today associate with the mid-life crisis —the late 30s and early 40s.

The responses of citizens and physicians to the conditions of living, hurting, and dying did undergo some important changes during these fifty years. The attention given yellow fever victims by physicians of this area was sophisticated for its day. There was also a concerted effort by one doctor, Ashbel Smith, to investigate the disease carefully by observation, experimentation, and dissection. Smith's report of 1839 was the first significant medical publication in the state. Almost forty years later, Greensville Dowell continued these "scientific" efforts with a lengthy historical survey of all the yellow fever epidemics afflicting Texans before 1876. Both physicians and citizens steadily rejected the hallowed therapies of bloodletting and purging. Galvestonians bought inexpensive proprietary medicines, but they also chose to be treated with the remedies of regular doctors who had modified their therapeutic practices considerably. Such was believed to be progress, and progress was celebrated.[52]

In 1869, Greensville Dowell inspired students at the Galveston Medical College with claims of great improvements that had occurred in medicine since his days as a student in the mid-1840s.[53] The new sciences of histology and cellular pathology had emerged because of improvements in the microscope. The use of general anesthetics had transformed the practice of surgery. Because of these improvements in medical science, Dowell claimed, life expectancy for Americans had increased from twenty-eight to forty-two years.

Others argued that better sanitation practices were the factors improving life expectancy. Since, for example, no one in Galveston really knew whether the epidemics of yellow fever were of local origin or were imported, citizens and physicians supported both sanitation efforts and quarantines. Who would deny that improvement of living conditions had not resulted from such efforts?

By the late 1860s, physicians in Galveston searched for ways to improve their professional effectiveness and their social distinctiveness. They organized a society, founded two medical schools, and established three medical journals, all within a twenty-year period. The expectations of the faculties at the medical colleges were of the highest order. Dr. N.A. Allen, of the Galveston Medical College, even went to Europe to acquire books and equipment for the college. The earliest medical journals in Texas were also remarkable, and the devotion of their editors extraordinary.

Throughout these fifty years, citizens and physicians cooperated in providing hospital care, not only for the poor and destitute, but for private-pay patients who were willing to receive care in the city hospital, St. Mary's Hospital, or the ones connected with the medical schools. The prepayment scheme of collecting a fee for passengers arriving from foreign countries to establish hospital care for transients may have been a unique system in the United States.

In recognizing the accomplishments and changes of these fifty years, we realize that it was no accident that the people of Texas, in 1881, voted to locate the medical department of its new state university in Galveston. But, state monies were not then available for new buildings. John Sealy, who died in 1884, requested that a portion of his estate be expended for "a charitable purpose."[54] It was also no accident that the executors of his estate chose to use this money for a new hospital that would serve the residents of the city, county, and state, and also enable construction of the university's medical school building, known today as Old Red.[55] Throughout its first half-century, patterns of concern about adequate medical care were a prominent feature of Galveston's social fabric.

Acknowledgement: For research assistance, I am especially grateful to two medical students, Mike Lifshen and Shawn Wright. For their help on numerous occasions, I wish to thank Inci Bowman and the Moody Medical Library staff, and Jane Kenamore and the Rosenberg Library staff.

Notes

1. Charles W. Hayes, *Galveston, History of the Island and the City* (Two volumes originally published in 1879; reprint by Jenkins Garrett Press, 1974), vol. 1, pp. 253-72, 289-92.
2. Ibid., 308-40.
3. Ibid., 341-45.

4. *Galveston Weekly News,* 5 Sept. 1854, p. 2, c. 2. Hereafter, this newspaper will be cited as *GWN.*

5. Ashbel Smith, *Yellow Fever in Galveston, Republic of Texas, 1839. An Account of the Great Epidemic,* ed. Chauncey D. Leake (Austin: University of Texas Press, 1951).

6. Hayes, vol. 1, p. 377.

7. Hayes, vol. 2, pp. 735-40; Greensville Dowell, *Yellow Fever and Malarial Diseases Embracing a History of the Epidemics of Yellow Fever in Texas* (Philadelphia: J. A. Moore, 1876).

8. *GWN,* 26 July 1859, p. 1, c. 1.

9. *Galveston Medical Journal* 2 (1867): 579. Hereafter, this journal will be cited as *GMJ.*

10. *GWN,* 15 February 1859, p. 3, c. 1.

11. *GWN,* 24 May 1859, p. 1, c. 2.

12. For example, see *GWN,* 6 May 1862, p. 1, c. 3.

13. Record of Interments of the City of Galveston, 1859-1872, copied by Peggy Gregory (Houston: Privately Printed, 1976).

14. Hayes, vol. 2, p. 736.

15. Smith, 51-52.

16. Ibid., 34.

17. *GWN,* 26 October 1858, p. 1, c. 1.

18. *GWN,* 7 September 1858, p. 1, c. 1.

19. *GWN,* 28 September 1858, p. 1, c. 7; 12 October 1858, p. 3, c. 1; 26 October 1858, p. 1, c. 5.

20. *GWN,* 8 May 1855, p. 1, c. 7.

21. *GWN,* 8 May 1855, p. 3, c. 3-5.

22. *GWN,* 15 May 1855, p. 2, c. 3-4.

23. *GWN,* 1 September 1857, p. 2, c. 1.

24. There are numerous reports in the *Galveston Medical Journal.* For examples, see 1 (1866): 417-30; 2 (1867): 935-37; 4 (1869): 510-13; 5 (1871): 358-59; 5 (1871): 364-68.

25. *GWN,* 7 September 1858, p. 1, c. 1.

26. Hayes, vol. 1, p. 342.

27. Ibid., 344.

28. Larry Wygant, "The Galveston Quarantine Stations, 1853-1950," *Texas Medicine,* 82 (June 1986): 49-52.

29. *GWN,* 2 June 1857, p. 3, c. 1.

30. *GWN,* 3 August 1858, p. 1, c. 1.

31. *Galveston Daily News,* 4 September 1875, p. 4, c. 3. Hereafter, this newspaper will be cited as *GDN.*

32. *GWN*, 2 November 1858, p. 2, c. 1.
33. Hayes, vol. 1, pp. 351, 360-61.
34. *The University of Texas Medical Branch at Galveston. A Seventy-Five Year History by the Faculty and Staff* (Austin: University of Texas Press, 1967), 4-5. Hereafter, this is cited as *UTMB 75 Year History*. Also see the Joseph Osterman Dyer Papers, which are located in the Galveston and Texas History Center of the Rosenberg Library in Galveston.
35. Joseph Osterman Dyer Papers, Box 1, File folder 14.
36. *GWN*, 28 December 1858, p. 3, c. 2.
37. *GDN*, 21 October 1865, p. 2, c. 2.
38. Supplement to *GDN*, 19 January 1873.
39. *GDN*, 24 February 1867, p. 3, c. 1.
40. Sister Mary Loyola Hegarty, *Serving with Gladness: The Origin and History of the Congregation of the Sisters of Charity of the Incarnate Word, Houston, Texas* (Houston: Bruce Pub. Co., 1967), 191-226.
41. *GMJ*, 1 (1866): 5-13.
42. Pat Ireland Nixon, *A History of the Texas Medical Association, 1853-1953* (Austin: University of Texas Press, 1953), 36-40.
43. Ibid., 71-76.
44. *UTMB 75 Year History*, 5-9 and Galveston Medical College, Faculty Minute Book, 18 May 1869, p. 101. This Minute Book is in the archives of the Moody Medical Library. The library is located on the campus of the University of Texas Medical Branch at Galveston.
45. *GMJ* 3 (1868): 562.
46. Galveston Medical College, Faculty Minute Book, 117-18.
47. *GMJ* 5 (1871): 344.
48. *GMJ* 3 (1868): 201.
49. *UTMB 75 Year History*, 9-10.
50. Inci Bowman, "Beginnings of Medical Journalism in Texas," *Texas Medicine* 82 (February 1986): 51-55.
51. *Texas Medical Journal* 1 (1873): 36.
52. Chester R. Burns, "Medicine in Texas: The Historical Literature," *Texas Medicine* 82 (January 1986): 60-63.
53. *GMJ* 5 (1870-71): 14-22.
54. *UTMB 75 Year History*, 15.
55. Kathleen M. Stephens, "Old Red: A Legacy Lives On," *Texas Medicine* 82 (April 1986): 50-53.

Abortion in Texas: Legal Enactments, Religious Traditions, and Social Hegemony

Harold Y. Vanderpool

Common wisdom once held that politics or religion should not be discussed in polite company. Since abortion raises both political and religious questions, this may be an exceedingly impolite essay—all the more so because abortion also embraces sensitive issues of human sexuality, male and female identity, family values, parent-child relationships, the social control of lawyers and the courts, and even views regarding race, poverty, and population control. This essay sketches the multi-faceted history of abortion legislation in the State of Texas in light of both the decisions of the U.S. Supreme Court and the roles of religious belief and commitment.

To understand this story we must, on the one hand, give particular attention to the impact of the famous *Roe v. Wade* decision of 1973—a court case that was initiated in Texas and had the effect of nullifying nearly all of the previous abortion statutes in Texas—as well as the statutes of many other states. On the other hand, we must attend to questions involving both the degrees to which religion does or does not influence what people think about abortion and the ways in which abortion became an issue around which Texans sought to establish self-identity and secure social power.

Legislation, 1854-1973

The story of legal enactments on abortion in the State of Texas begins in February of 1854, when the Texas legislature first passed criminal abortion statutes. These statutes were passed when the legislatures of several states had become alarmed over various issues surrounding induced abortion. These issues included concern over the harms inflicted on women by self-elected, non-M.D. abortionists, over the increasingly widespread use of abortion to control family size, over the falling birth rates of Anglo-Saxon Americans vis-à-vis Irish Catholics and other immigrants, and over the increasing dissemination of contraceptive information through the U.S. mails.[1] Prior to the middle decades of the nineteenth century, little abortion ferment had arisen in America. In the 1820s and 1830s, for example, abortions were frequently obtained by American women from physicians who were informed about terminating unwanted pregnancies and had few qualms of conscience in assisting their patients. The vast majority of Americans at the time did not view abortion before quickening—that is, before the fetus moves in the mother's womb some four months after impregnation—as immoral; nor did English and American common law recognize abortion before quickening as a criminal offense. Popular belief held that the fetus began to gain some semblance of separate existence only after quickening, at which time the certainty of pregnancy was far more easily determined.[2]

The enactments of the Texas legislature in 1854 sought to balance common-law tradition with rising concerns over the frequency of abortion, over falling fertility rates, and so on. The Texas legislature thus made abortion *after quickening* a crime carrying up to ten years in prison. These criminal penalties for abortion after quickening applied only to abortionists, not to self-attempted abortions by pregnant women. The legislature set forth a newly-revised Texas code in 1856 that reduced prison sentences for the crime to between two and five years. The code also added clauses that defined abortion-related deaths of the expectant mother as murder, that declared that those who furnished abortifacients were accomplices to the crime, and that stated that therapeutic abortions (abortion "for the purpose of saving the life of the woman") were exempt from criminal prosecution.[3] Within two more years, an additional statute stated that any abortion *attempt*, regardless of its success, was also a crime.[4]

By 1866 a significant new change was made in Texas law, a change that completed the state's legislative enactments on abortion until they would be struck down almost completely over a century later in *Roe v. Wade*. This change involved dropping out quickening or "quick with child" as the critical beginning point for defining criminal abortion. Instead, an intentional interruption of pregnancy *at any time* was declared a crime. The Texas law thus read,

> If any person shall designedly administer to a pregnant woman . . . any drug or medicine, or shall use towards her any violence, or any means whatever, externally or internally applied, and thusly procure an abortion, he shall be punished, by confinement, in the penitentiary, not less than two, or more than five years.[5]

This change was in keeping with similar ones made by thirty other states between 1866 and 1877.[6]

The reasons for the resurgence in anti-abortion legislation after the Civil War were many. First, a fervent anti-abortion crusade was mounted by physician members of the American Medical Association. These doctors were determined to squeeze out quacks or irregular physicians, to gain greater professional recognition and public prestige, to protect the lives of women whose lives were often seriously jeopardized by abortions, and to protect fetal life.[7] Second, many white, native-born Protestant Americans were increasingly worried and alarmed that Catholics, who did not accept abortion, were out-producing them. Third, male fears over changing traditional roles of females generally and their own wives particularly, fueled attempts to maintain pregnancies so as to keep women more closely confined to homemaking roles.[8] And finally, Republican reconstruction governments after the Civil War sought to systematize and professionalize social policy.[9]

Notably, the doctors who led in this anti-abortion legislative campaign had little help from organized religion throughout the period from 1860 to 1880. Not until 1869 did Catholics and Congregationalists (Protestant churches descending from the Puritans) begin to speak out against abortion. Presbyterians were the first major American Protestant denomination to take an anti-abortion stand on the national level.[10] This occurred when the Old and New School Presbyterians united in 1870, and declared that

> [T]he destruction by parents of their own offspring, before birth. . . [is] a crime against God and against nature. . . . we whereby warn those that are guilty of this crime that, except they repent, they cannot inherit eternal life.[11]

This position represented a recovery of the anti-abortion views of Martin Luther, John Calvin, and other major founders of the Protestant Reformation. Their opposition to induced abortion exceeded that of their Catholic contemporaries, because their stand on abortion reflected characteristic Protestant theological emphases on original sin and total depravity. By holding that each human conceptus from the beginning of its existence directly bears the full humanity of its parents, Luther and other reformers underscored how each generation inherited, then passed along, the original sin and depravity of Adam.[12] Abortion thereby amounted to both the murder and eternal damnation of each yet-unborn individual.

On the basis of this legacy, why had not American Protestants opposed abortion prior to 1870? They did not do so for at least two reasons. First, beginning with the Puritans, the beliefs of American Protestants were informed by the Bible as much as by writings and creeds of their historic founders. In turn, the Bible does not sustain strong anti-abortion beliefs. In fact, the Bible does not expressly mention abortion, and in the one instance where miscarriage is discussed (Exodus 21:22), does not regard the expelled fetus as equal to a living human. Second, beginning in the early decades of the nineteenth century, mainline Protestant traditions in America revised and pruned away earlier notions of original sin, total depravity, and predestination.[13] In the process, they by and large lost touch with the anti-abortion legacies of their forbearers. Therefore, when Protestants began joining ranks with the physician-led anti-abortion campaign, they did so not because they were recovering their historic theological legacies, but because they too were beginning to worry about greater Catholic birthrates, about the greater "love of pleasure and of ease . . . [and] perverted views of life" in the late Victorian era, and were responding to the pressure of anti-abortionist doctors.[14] For over one hundred years the Texas laws of 1866 and the medical and religious traditions that supported them were to hold sway in the state.

Roe v. Wade (1973)

In 1970, events in Texas began to unfold that were eventually to give rise to our present laws and resultant controversies. In that year, a single pregnant woman—whom the court assigned the pseudonym Jane Roe in order to protect her privacy—brought suit against Henry Wade, the district attorney of Dallas County. Ms. Roe—now recognized as Norma McCorvey—claimed that the Texas state abortion statute was unconstitutional. After two years of hearing arguments on the case, the U.S. Supreme Court in January of 1973 made its decision: the laws of Texas, along with those of a majority of states, were in conflict with the constitutional right of privacy. The Court specified that two additional legal principles should shape abortion law—the right of states to protect maternal health and the right of states to protect developing life. By way of balancing these three legal principles, the majority opinion of the Supreme Court divided the period of human gestation or pregnancy into three periods or trimesters.[15] In the first trimester the right of a pregnant woman to terminate a pregnancy, subject to consultation with her doctor, was held supreme. In practice, most physicians did not question the right of American women to terminate pregnancy in the first three months. After twelve weeks, the fetus is some three-and-one-half inches long; its organs are present, its brain structure is developed, and its heartbeat can be heard.[16]

In the second trimester, states can insist upon reasonable standards of medical care if an abortion is attempted. In the third trimester (months seven through nine) the premature infant is more and more "viable," that is, it can live outside the mother's womb by means of artificial aids. At the end of seven months, some ten percent of premature infants can survive, and they weigh about two pounds.[17] The Court held that when the fetus became viable, a state's "legitimate interest in potential life" can override the pregnant woman's right of privacy and self-determination "except when it is necessary to preserve the life or health of the mother."[18] In other words, for the last three months of pregnancy, the Court essentially upheld the laws on the books forbidding abortions save for threats to the mother's life. Aware of the history of abortion legislation, Justice Blackmun, speaking for six of his colleagues, rightly observed that "at the time of the adoption of our Constitution, and throughout the major portion of the nineteenth century. . . a woman enjoyed a substantially broader right to terminate a pregnancy" than was the case in most states in 1973.[19] However new and revolutionary the Court's decision seemed in 1973, it was in part reinstating past common-law traditions.

Like the changes in Texas statutes earlier, the *Roe v. Wade* abortion decision rested upon important social, medical, philosophical, and religious foundations. It did not, that is, emerge full-blown from the mind of Justice Blackmun. Background developments underlying *Roe v. Wade* included at least eight factors. First, in light of medical advances, former reasons for prohibiting abortions on grounds that they were more dangerous to a woman's health than her carrying the fetus-infant to term were no longer valid for the first months of pregnancy.[20] Second, *Roe v. Wade* rested on legal research and history, which indicated that the status of personhood, citizenship, and rights rests upon being born and alive. As accented in the majority opinion of the Court, American law never regarded embryos or fetuses as equal to the mother. Had this been the case, no doctor could have tried to save a mother's life by an abortion without both a due process trial for the fetus and a charge against the woman as an accomplice to the crime.[21] Third, as *Roe v. Wade* points out, American religious opinion was sharply divided at the time—sometimes fervently against and sometimes fervently for the woman's right to choose, as well as fervently for or against a belief in the "personhood" or ensoulment of the zygote and/or fetus.[22] Fourth, in the years prior to 1973, worries over overpopulation gave rise to general concern regarding greater regulation of offspring and birth control. Increased support for contraceptive research resulted in the approval of the "pill" by the FDA in 1960, as well as to increased funding for voluntary sterilization.[23] Fifth, a significant majority of doctors seemed to favor a change in state abortion regulations.[24]

Sixth, the women's movement of the 1960s and 1970s increasingly and strongly advocated that women should have inalienable rights of control over procreation. The court gave evidence regarding this pressure, yet specifically denied that *Roe v. Wade* amounted to abortion on demand.[25] Seventh, many women were in fact procuring abortions (between 200,000 and 1,200,000 annually in the 1960s), and widespread sentiment held that in part this gave rise to a travesty of justice. Wealthy women generally had access to private and, if necessary, out-of-state clinics with high medical standards, while poorer and minority women did not.[26] Eighth, between 1968 and 1973 thirteen states had in fact liberalized their abortion laws. Most of these permitted abortion in order to safeguard the physical and mental health of pregnant women, in order to enable women not to have to carry mentally or physically handicapped infants to term, and in order to enable victims of rape or incest to terminate their pregnancies. Before 1973, the states of Alaska, Hawaii, and Washington had so completely eliminated all restrictions for "medically indicated abortion" that they were relatively untouched by *Roe v. Wade*.[27]

As *Vernon's Annotated Revised Civil Statutes of the State of Texas* of 1976 notes, *Roe v. Wade* nullified all but one of Texas' abortion statutes. This statute forbade the destruction of a child "being born" but before actual birth, meaning that live infants after being aborted were protected. The statute stipulated that this crime is punishable by not less than five years in the penitentiary.[28] The revised statutes furthermore expressly point out that except for the "being born" article "there are no laws in this state regulating abortion *per se*."[29] *Roe v. Wade* did not declare third-trimester abortions illegal, but held, rather, that, except in instances where maternal life and health were threatened, states have the *power* to so declare. Unlike many other states that enacted statutes prohibiting nontherapeutic, third-trimester abortions, Texas instituted no such laws.[30] Public responses to *Roe v. Wade* reflected the highly emotional character of abortion, over which Americans were sharply divided. A Gallup Poll taken a year before the release of the Court's decision indicated that sixty-six percent of Americans favored "liberalized" abortion laws—reflecting almost exactly the views of physicians one year after the decision.[31] Among those who rejoiced over the justices' decisions in *Roe v. Wade* were numerous persons whose views were represented by civil liberty organizations, women's rights groups, and the Protestant-sponsored National Council of Churches. Led initially by Catholics, opposing organizations immediately voiced alarm and consternation and warned of coming holocausts and a devaluing of life that would end in the deaths of the elderly and infirm.[32]

From Roe v. Wade to the Present

The alarm and outrage of active opponents to *Roe v. Wade* soon resulted in state laws designed to roll back the effects of that historic decision. Some of these laws required that women secure the consent of their husbands before an abortive procedure.[33] Others stipulated that the doctor must personally secure the woman's informed consent, that is, tell her "just what would be done and . . . its consequences."[34] Others required a waiting period after the woman's initial visit to the doctor.[35] Some statutes provided that the woman should be given specific information about her fetus' stage of development,[36] as well as information pertaining to abortion alternatives.[37] Still other state statutes required that all abortions be performed in hospitals,[38] the average costs of which in the first three months ($735 in 1982) were about four times greater than in clinics ($190 in 1981).[39] Certain states proceeded to require protection of fetal life prior to viability.[40]

The most active of the groups opposing *Roe v. Wade* was and is the National Right to Life Committee (NRLC) with its respective state and city branches. Approximately seventy percent of NRLC members are Catholic. Sixty-three percent are women, eighty-seven percent married, ninety-eight percent white; and the majority represent solidly middle-income bracket families ($20,000-$40,000 per year).[41] Other pro-life groups include the Christian Action Council, the Conservative Caucus, the Moral Majority, the Religious Round Table, and the National Council of Roman Catholic Bishops. Several of these groups expressly target their activism toward the U.S. Congress,[42] and have received strong support from the Republican party at the national level.

Momentously, eight months prior to the *Roe v. Wade* decision, President Nixon began bringing the issue of abortion into national politics by declaring that he opposed liberalized abortion laws and by speaking of the need to protect unborn children. Three years later, opponents of abortion had mustered the strength to pressure presidential candidates to state their position on the matter—a politicizing measure that ended in the Republican Party's national platform of 1976 expressing resentment toward federal "intrusions on abortions."[43]

The Party's 1984 platform called for the appointment of judges at all levels "who respect traditional family values and the sanctity of human life." Conversely, the Democratic platform that year spoke in favor of "reproductive freedom as a fundamental human right."[44]

In spite of activism and opposition, nearly all of the above post-*Roe v. Wade* legislative actions were declared unconstitutional at either a circuit or

Supreme Court level. In *Planned Parenthood v. Danforth* (1976), the Supreme Court struck down all state requirements for a husband's consent, reasoning that if states do not have the power to veto a woman's abortion, surely a husband does not.[45] *Danforth* furthermore forbade any blanket requirement of a parent's or guardian's approval for an unmarried minor's abortion request.[46] In 1976 the Sixth Circuit Court ruled that the law does not recognize fetal rights or the necessity of protecting fetal life before viability.[47] This decision and the law's focus on viability was reaffirmed by the U.S. Supreme Court in *Colautti v. Franklin* (1979), which called viability "the critical point."[48] This view was reaffirmed once again in the landmark 1983 *City of Akron v. Akron Center for Reproductive Health.* In *City of Akron,* the Court reaffirmed the position in *Roe v. Wade* "that a State may not adopt a single theory as to when life begins to justify its regulations of abortion."[49]

City of Akron was pivotal for several reasons. By defending the principles set forth in *Roe v. Wade* against state laws designed to blunt their effects, *City* both endorsed a decade of Supreme Court rulings and eased worries of those who were thinking that recent decisions over not requiring Medicaid funding for abortions signaled a change of direction by the Court.[50]

Specifically, *City* placed an even stronger emphasis on the woman's right of choice than that found in *Roe v. Wade. Roe v. Wade* had expressly rejected the right of each woman to terminate her pregnancy when, how, and as she wished, and instead called abortion "inherently, and primarily, a medical decision" for the doctor to make in consultation with the pregnant patient.[51] In keeping with their own traditional images of the roles and values of doctors, the justices had reasoned that physicians would keep *Roe v. Wade* from amounting to "abortion on demand."[52] *City,* however, interpreted *Roe v. Wade* as a "full vindication of the woman's fundamental right" to an abortion and as commissioning doctors with "assisting the woman in the decision-making process and implementing her decision should she choose abortion."[53]

The various legislative attempts to escape the effects of *Roe v. Wade* that were struck down in *City of Akron* included the following: laws requiring that patients be told specifics about fetal development and characteristics, laws requiring that physicians personally counsel with patients (*City* held that other qualified professionals can do this), laws requiring a waiting period between the time a woman receives information about an abortion and undergoes the procedure, and laws requiring that abortions be performed in hospitals.[54] State laws requiring hospitalized care for early abortions were viewed as unnecessary for safety and as placing unnecessary and unjust financial, travel, and time constraints on those seeking to exercise their constitutional rights.[55]

As noted previously, although given the right to do so by the U.S. Supreme Court, the State of Texas did not pass legislation regulating abortions in the second and third trimesters of a woman's pregnancy. Texas did, however, pass legislation protecting individuals and institutions who are conscientiously opposed to performing abortions. In 1977, articles were added to the State's legal statutes that granted individuals and private hospitals the right of private conscience either to perform or not perform abortions without being civilly liable, being denied public funding, or suffering from discrimination.[56] Likewise, students and employees of Texas educational institutions were not to be denied admission or employment because of qualms of conscience over abortion. Lest the State be ruled as interfering with a woman's decision to abort, however, public hospitals were required to honor legally acceptable abortion requests.[57]

As with other states, Texas' consent requirements for the medical treatment of minors appear to be out of step with post-*Roe v. Wade* rulings by the U.S. Supreme Court. The State of Texas Family Code defines a minor as a person under eighteen years of age who is not or has not been married and who has not been declared an adult by court order. The State holds that a minor's consent alone is an insufficient warrant for medical treatment, but rather, that a parent, guardian, or, in cases where these parties cannot be contacted, another officially recognized person or institution (grandparent, school that has obtained an official authorization, and so on) must render substituted consent for the minor.[58] Exceptions to minors being incapable of consenting to treatment are spelled out in the Texas Family Code: a minor's consent is sufficient if the minor is on active military duty, is sixteen or older and living apart from parents or guardian, or is receiving medical treatment related to pregnancy, *except treatment for abortion*.

Interestingly, the "except for abortion" aspect of the Texas Family Code was precisely the point of controversy in two Supreme Court rulings. In *Planned Parenthood v. Danforth* (1976) the Court held that contrary to existing laws in the State of Missouri, no blanket consent requirement for abortion by an unmarried minor's parents could be required by a state. Parental rights to veto a teenage daughter's abortion were regarded in *Danforth* as infringing on the constitutional rights of minors—rights that should not be denied them. Nor did the Court accept the notion that parental ties are improved by giving parents such veto powers.[59] Three years later in *Belloti v. Baird* (1979) the Supreme Court ruled—versus ordinances in the State of Massachusetts—that minors are not required to notify and consult with parents, but rather, can go directly to a court for an independent judicial judgment. The court would then determine whether the minor is mature enough to give her own consent apart from parental influence.

These sensitive and controversial rulings, passed in the midst of social turmoil and increasing numbers of teenage pregnancies, strongly suggest that any imposition of a blanket parental consent requirement—as in the Texas Family Code—is unconstitutional.[60] It thus appears that unemancipated minors (those still living with their parents) who are mature and well-informed enough to make a decision can do so—meaning that doctors who perform abortions in the first trimester for such minors would not be held liable for civil damages. These cases, however, are highly charged, and include the likelihood of distress and anger from protective parents. While some lawyers counsel doctors to obtain the consent of parents or guardians in these circumstances, others suggest that the consent of mature minors is sufficiently set forth in federal legislation to protect physicians.[61] Given the significance of the notion of "mature" minors in *Danforth* and *Belloti* and the role of the courts in determining which minors can give valid consent in *Belloti*, doctors who have questions as to a minor's maturity will be wise to seek a court's judgment.

Religion, Abortion, and Texas' Religious Profile

The above sketch of abortion legislation in the State of Texas indicates how religious traditions served as a backdrop for public opinion and responses to changing law. This sketch, however, does not provide us with insights into the more particular dynamics and roles of Texas' religious traditions with respect to changing abortion law. By way of exploring these dynamics and roles, we should note at the outset that social science surveys show that religious affiliation and commitment are "the most dominating variables" for attitudes and feelings regarding abortion. Religion, that is, exceeds in importance such demographic and political variables as social class, race, education, and sex.[62] At the same time, religious affiliation includes not one, but a cluster of characteristic factors, including an ideological perspective about God, human nature, and the natural world; gender identity and roles; ethnic traditions; social class; and psychological orientation towards authority figures, a sense of belonging to a group, and one's sense of personal independence.[63] In short, religious traditions represent clusters of values and orientations that, naturally, are held all the more fervently by those who are most active in each tradition.

More particularly, profiles of the ardent activists behind either pro-choice or anti-abortion ("pro-life") positions illustrate how religion clearly interdigitates with attitudes about abortion. Pro-choice members of the National Abortion Rights Action League consisted in 1980 of mainline Protestants (25%) (including Episcopalians, Methodists, and Presbyterians) Jews (17%), a sprinkling of Catholics (4%), and many self-described agnostics (25%) and atheists (15%). In contrast, the pro-life National Right to Life Committee was comprised of Catholics by a clear majority (70%), a number of Protestants (20%) (mostly conservative Baptists, Lutherans, and other evangelicals), and a few Jews (.5%), atheists (1%), and agnostics (.5%).[64]

Regarding Texas' religious profile, in 1980 slightly over fifty percent of Texas' population of 14,229,000 belonged to the ten largest religious groups in the state. This means, of course, that almost half of the residents of Texas were not affiliated with a particular religious group—a finding reaffirmed in 1988.[65] In order of their size, the largest religious traditions in Texas in 1980 included Southern Baptists (2,660,000 adherents), Catholics (2,340,000), United Methodists (932,000), the Churches of Christ (355,000), Presbyterians (182,000), Episcopalians (175,000), the Assemblies of God (162,000), Disciples of Christ (120,000), Missouri Synod Lutherans (117,000), and American Lutherans (107,000).[66] Of course, variety exists within each of these groups. There are not a few Bourbon-drinking Baptists, lukewarm Church of Christers, and Presbyterians who hardly know how fervently John Calvin believed in predestination. It is likely that a similar level of diversity exists with respect to views on abortion within each of these denominations.

Consider certain differences between Texas' two largest denominations, both of which now line up on the anti-abortion or pro-life side of the ledger. Studies have shown that Baptists and Catholics who attend church most frequently are more likely *not to approve* of abortion. At the same time Baptists (but not Catholics) with higher educations are significantly more likely *to approve* of abortion.[67] Baptists, other evangelicals, and Catholics are far more likely to become anti-abortion activists if they also hold to conservative views of marriage and sexuality—for example, if they are opposed to sex education in schools, favor stricter divorce laws, and voice opposition to pre-marital and extra-marital sex.[68]

Catholics differ more on abortion than many Americans realize. True, the official pronouncements of church officials from Texas Catholic dioceses maintain that abortion for the directly intended purpose of terminating pregnancy "is never permitted."[69] Yet, Catholicism's seam is divided. Gallup and Harris polls in 1979, for example, show that twenty-one percent of American Catholics believed that abortion should be legal in all circumstances—compared to twenty-three percent of Protestants and twenty-six percent of Americans in general, and fifty-two percent of Catholics believed in legalized abortions in certain circumstances—versus sixty percent of Protestants and fifty-four percent of Americans generally.[70] A New York State survey of Catholic clergy at the end of 1973 indicated that thirty-two percent of those surveyed disagreed with or had doubts about traditional church teaching on abortion (i.e., 68% agreed with official church teaching). Of the clergy with doctorate degrees between the ages of twenty-five and forty-four, only thirty-seven percent said they completely agreed with the churchs' official teaching.[71] Thus, even though the Catholic church in America continues to take a strong pro-life position, its own ranks are far from united—a fact made clear during the 1984 presidential campaign.[72]

The next largest religious group in Texas that opposes abortion is the Church of Christ, the conservative wing of the Disciples of Christ or Campbellite tradition. Given its strong emphasis on congregational autonomy, as well as the scanty and debatable references to abortion in the Bible, the Churches of Christ do not have an official position on abortion, pro or con. But similar to Southern Baptists, the Churches of Christ now lean toward a pro-life point of view, while encompassing other positions.[73]

Most of the remaining ten largest religious groups in Texas are mainline Protestant traditions—Methodists, Presbyterians, Lutherans, and Episcopalians—which, together with the Disciples of Christ or Christian Churches, include over 1.5 million Texans (11% of the state's population). In keeping with their respective national pronouncements on abortions, most of these traditions favor a moderate pro-choice stance, while recognizing and supporting religious and cultural pluralism.[74] Through such prominent educational institutions as Southern Methodist University and Texas Christian University, the influence of these traditions likely exceeds their numbers.

Religion, Self-Identity, and Social Power

The preceding insights and profile shed light on the dynamics and roles of religion vis-à-vis the historic changes of abortion legislation in Texas. That sketch indicated that the initial laws restricting abortion were set forth at a time when doctors were seeking to squeeze out quacks and irregular physicians, when men were becoming worried over the changing roles of their wives and other women, and when white, native-born Protestants were becoming alarmed that they were being out-produced by Catholics and other immigrants. In short, the impetus for Texas' initial and restrictive statutes regarding induced abortion stemmed from fears over the loss of traditional patterns of control, or, put a bit more positively, by efforts to maintain cultural hegenomy on the part of well-entrenched groups within the population.

Struggles over social control ensued again in the period just prior to *Roe v. Wade* when several states liberalized their abortion laws. New York's laws, for example, were decriminalized in 1970—in keeping with the views of a majority of that state's leaders and citizens.[75] In contrast, the concerted effort to introduce a moderate "Humane Abortions" bill in Texas in 1969 failed. The bill itself carefully circumscribed the conditions—rape, incest, and grave impairments of a woman's physical or mental health—under which a "Humane Abortion [Hospital] Committee" might approve of abortion. Its supporters included the American Medical Association, the United Presbyterian Church, the Lutheran Churches of America, the Unitarian Universalist Association, and the Union of American Hebrew Congregations.[76] Having failed to achieve their objectives in the Texas Legislature, these groups and the Texans they represented were, in effect, granted social power by the Supreme Court justices in *Roe v. Wade*. Moreover, under the banners of freedom, compassion, justice, and a decade of progressive change in America, these persons believed they deserved the cultural hegenomy bequeathed to them.

While pro-choice Texans did not constitute a majority of the state's population,[77] exceedingly widespread sympathy in the state favored liberalized abortion laws. Even Southern Baptists in their annual convention of 1971 declared that they would

> work for legislation that will allow the possibility of abortion under such conditions as rape, incest, clear evidence of severe fetal deformity, and carefully ascertained evidence of the likelihood of damage to the emotional, mental and physical health of the mother.[78]

This view reflected general Baptist sentiment and the opinions of prominent church leaders. A poll of devout Southern Baptists in 1969 revealed, for example, that sixty-eight percent favored "liberalized" abortion laws. And even W.A. Criswell, pastor of the First Baptist Church of Dallas, who in recent years has warmly befriended the anti-abortion cause, said in 1973 that he "always felt" that the mother's best interest should be honored because the fetus was not "an individual person" before birth.[79] Progressive Texans, religiously affiliated or otherwise, thus took stands on abortion in keeping with their self-images as leaders responsible for all the state's citizens. Their positions on abortion served to symbolize their commitment to such values as broadened civil liberties in the face of greater cultural pluralism—including the rights of women to make decisions in accordance with their own consciences, more sex education, greater levels of control over family size and early pregnancy, and concern for the plight and well-being of the poor.[80] These values resonated precisely with many of the major themes and trends of Protestant theology in the 1960s and early 1970s.[81]

Meanwhile, tired of being criticized and browbeaten, American conservatives began resisting mightily the power and authority of their progressive and liberal adversaries. Although their political ambitions were empowered by the phalanx they formed around the candidacy, then presidency, of Ronald Reagan, they sought to gain influence in numerous organizations. To use Baptists as a weathervane for conservative Protestant opinion, over the course of the decade following *Roe v. Wade*, Southern Baptist fundamentalists espousing the infallibility of the Bible effectively seized the leadership of the entire denomination. In the process, many moderate scholars, administrators, and preachers were designated "liberals" and either pushed to the side or out of positions of leadership in the denomination.

Notably, the denomination's pronouncements on abortion matched step for step this power shift. Having declared that they would work for a liberalization of abortion laws in 1971, Texas Baptists resolved in their annual convention of 1974 that they abhorred "the widespread practice...commercialization and exploitation" of abortion.[82] Two years later the convention lamented the Supreme Court's *Danforth* decision "which limits the authority of parents over their minor children."[83] By 1980 the convention adopted a distinctly anti-abortion stance that called for "legislation prohibiting abortion except to save the life of the mother or in the case of incest or rape."[84] And by 1984 the once progressive Baptist convention voted for a "constitutional amendment which will prohibit abortion except to save the physical life of the mother."[85]

What forces empowered this quick and dramatic reversal by Texas' Southern Baptists? What caused these fundamentalists to turn a blind eye to the articulate defenses of a moderate pro-abortion stance by their fellow Baptists in universities and colleges,[86] and, against the grain of centuries of antipathy, embrace the precise position of alarmed and outspoken Catholic traditionalists?[87] It appears that once again in Texas history abortion served as a vehicle for the conveying and wielding of social power. By identifying with Right-to-Life organizations on a national scale and, more particularly, with the conservative political constituency of President Reagan, fundamentalist Baptists and other evangelicals in Texas sought and secured greater visibility and credibility. Their stand on abortion served as a graphic cultural symbol, on the surface of which were no specific theological disputes, but an acceptance of which conveyed an entire set of prioritized values. These included first-order commitments to the sanctity of life, marriage, and the family—in contrast to the prioritized values of personal liberty, justice, self-growth, social change, and cultural pluralism by liberals. "Pro-life" became shorthand language for an opposition to sex and cohabitation before marriage, for stricter divorce laws, for tight limits on public sex education, and for a devotion to traditional, family roles for women and leadership roles for men.[88]

Behind this quest for power by conservatives lay a search for security in face of the upheavals in the 1960s and 1970s—upheavals over freedom of sexual expression, over women's roles, over traditional forms of authority, and, of course, over the Vietnam war. Shocked by these and yet again by the number of abortions and the quick rise of the new, profit-oriented abortion clinics following *Roe v. Wade*,[89] Christian traditionalists became acutely concerned that the dismantling of abortion laws—like those that once regulated alcohol consumption, divorce, birth control, and consenting adult sexual relationships decades before—represented a further and disastrous loss of cultural hegemony.[90] Not since the Prohibition era had such contention and maneuvering swarmed around a sensitive question of personal morality in America. It remains to be seen whether, similar to the Prohibition era from 1918 to 1933, the personal morality of some will once more be declared by legislation and law the public morality for all.

Notes

1. James C. Mohr, *Abortion in America* (New York: Oxford University Press, 1978), 83-139.
2. William J. Curran, "An Historical Perspective on the Law of Personality and Status with Special Regard to the Human Fetus and the Rights of Women," *Milbank Memorial Fund Quarterly* 61 (Winter 1983): 58-75; Mohr, 3-19.
3. See George W. Paschal, *A Digest of the Laws of Texas,* 2d. ed. (Washington, D.C.: W.H. and D.H. Morrison, 1870), 447.
4. Mohr, 139.
5. Paschal, 447; compare with wording in *Roe v. Wade* in *Supreme Court Register* 93 (1974), 709, note 1.

6. Mohr, 200.
7. Ibid., 148-66.
8. Speaking to a male audience, the leading anti-abortionist physician of the period, Horatio Storer, once remarked that he wanted each woman to loose some of her chains, "to increase her health, prolong her life . . . in a word, selfishly to enhance her values to ourselves." Storer also said that he wanted women to stay in "their proper and God-given sphere," not "the pulpit, the forum, or cares of state, nor. . . the practice of medical profession." Ibid., 168-69.
9. Ibid., 167-70, 203 ff.
10. Ibid., 186-91.
11. Ibid., 192.
12. James B. Nelson, "Abortion: Protestant Perspectives," in *Encyclopedia of Bieothics,* ed. Warren T. Reich (New York: Free Press, 1978), 14.
13. H. Shelton Smith, *Changing Concepts of Original Sin in America* (New York: Scribner's, 1955).
14. Mohr, 188-95, quotation from 189.
15. 410 U.S. 113 (1973).
16. Hellegers, "The Beginning of Life," in *Contemporary Issues in Bioethics,* ed. Tom L. Beauchamp and LeRoy Walters (Encino, Calif.: Dickenson, 1978), 197.
17. Hellegers, 197.
18. *Supreme Court Reporter,* vol. 93, p. 732.
19. Ibid., 720.
20. Ibid., vol. 93, pp. 724-25; and Mohr, 253-54.
21. 410 U.S. 116 (1973), section IX with footnotes 54 and 55. See also Curran.
22. Leonard J. Nelson III, "The Churches and Abortion Law Reform," *Journal of Christian Jurisprudence* 29 (1983): 29-56; *Roe v. Wade,* 410 U.S. 116 (1973), section IX.
23. Mohr, 250-51.
24. Ibid., 252-53 and 255-56. Also *Supreme Court Reporter,* vol. 93, p. 722.
25. *Supreme Court Reporter,* vol. 93, p. 727, and Mohr, 253.
26. Mohr, 254-55.
27. B. J. George, Jr., "State Legislation *versus* the Supreme Court: Abortion Legislation in the 1980's," *Pepperdine Law Review* 12 (1985): 441-42.
28. *Vernon's Annotated Revised Civil Statutes of the State of Texas,* vol. 13 (St. Paul, Minn.: West Publishing, 1976), 224-25.
29. Ibid., 245.
30. Terry O. Tottenham et al., "Texas Abortion Law: Consent Requirements and Special Statutes," *Houston Law Review* 18 (May 1981): 228.

31. Harold L. Hirsh, "Impact of the Supreme Court Decisions on the Performance of Abortions in the United States," *Forensic Science* 3 (1974): 219.
32. "Abortion Decision, A Death Blow?" *Christianity Today* (19 February 1973): 48.
33. George, 445-46.
34. Ibid., 458.
35. Ibid., 480.
36. Ibid., 461-62.
37. Ibid., 260-61.
38. Ibid., 506-10.
39. Stanley K. Henshaw, "Freestanding Abortion Clinics: Services, Structure, Fees," *Family Planning Perspectives* 14 (September/October 1982): 248-56.
40. George, 445-46, and Tottenham, 826-27 and 841-43.
41. Donald Granberg, "Abortion Activists," *Family Planning Perspectives* 13 (July/August 1981): 157-63.
42. Paul D. Simmons, "Fundamentalism and the Politics of Abortion," unpublished ms., 1981.
43. Mohr, 260; and Eva R. Rubin, *Abortion, Politics, and the Courts* (Westport, Conn.: Greenwood Press, 1982), 87 ff.
44. George, 428, note 3.
45. Ibid., 468; and Tottenham, 823-29.
46. 428 U.S., 74.
47. Tottenham, 826.
48. Ibid., 841.
49. 51 L.W. 4767, section V-A.
50. George J. Annas, "*Roe v. Wade* Reaffirmed," *The Hastings Center Report* 14 (August 1983): 21-22.
51. 410 U.S. 116, section VIII; and William J. Winslade and Judith Wilson Ross, "The Courts and Medical Decisions: Unhappy Parallels Between the Abortion Problem and Babies Doe," unpublished ms.
52. William J. Curran, "The Abortion Decisions," *The New England Journal of Medicine* 288 (3 May 1973): 950-51; and James H. Ford, "Mass Produced, Assembly-Line Abortion," *California Medicine* 117 (November 1972): 80-84.
53. 51 L W 4767, section II.
54. 51 L W 4767, section III.
55. 51 L W 4767.
56. *Vernon's Texas Statutes and Codes* (St. Paul, Minn.: West Publishing Co., 1982), article 45 12.7.

57. Tottenham, 845-47.
58. Texas Family Code, section 35.01-35.03 (Vernon, 1975); and M. G. Young, Jr., "Medicine and the Law: Treatment of Minors—Consent Requirements," *Texas Medicine* 79 (January 1983): 72-73.
59. 428 U.S. 52 (1976); and Rubin, 130-32.
60. Tottenham, 834.
61. Compare Tottenham, 834, with Young, 73.
62. Jerome S. Legge, Jr., "The Determinants of Attitudes Toward Abortion in the American Electorate," *Western Political Quarterly* 36 (1983): 479-90, quotation from 487; and Donald Granberg, "The Abortion Activists," 157-63.
63. See the brief "primer on religion" and its bibliography in Jeffrey S. Levin and Harold Y. Vanderpool, "Is Frequent Religious Attendance *Really* Conducive to Better Health?: Toward an Epidemiology of Religion," *Social Science and Medicine* 24 (1987): 589-600.
64. Granberg, "Abortion Activists," 160.
65. Anonymous, "Churchgoer Decline Worries Baptists," *The Galveston Daily News* (25 January 1988): 3-B.
66. Mike Kingston, ed., *Texas Almanac* (Dallas: A. H. Belo Corp., 1985), 629.
67. Donald Granberg and Beth Wellman Granberg, "Abortion Attitudes, 1965-1980: Trends and Determinants," *Family Planning Perspectives* 12 (September/October 1980): 250-61, esp. 258.
68. Granberg, "Abortion Activists," 162.
69. Texas Medical Association, 32-33.
70. "Eighty Percent of Americans . . . ," *Family Planning Perspectives* 11 (May/June 1979): 189-90.
71. Frank J. Traina, "Catholic Clergy on Abortion," *Family Planning Perspectives* 6 (Summer 1974): 151-56.
72. John Herbers, "Scholars Say Church's Abortion is not Monolithic," *New York Times* (15 September 1984): 29.
73. See "Church Leaders Discuss Abortion Issue," *Christian Chronicle* 43 (February 1986): 4.
74. Texas Medical Association, 13, 23, 44; and George, 429-30.
75. Estimations are that in 1969, 52.5 percent of New Yorkers believed that pregnant women should have the right to an abortion upon request—versus 37.4 percent opposed. Eric M. Uslaner and Ronald E. Weber, "Public Support for Pro-Choice Abortion Policies in the Nation and States," in *The Law and Politics*, ed. Carl E. Schneider and Maris A. Vinovskis (Lexington, Mass.: D. C. Heath, 1980), 218.
76. Texas H.B. 323 (1969).

77. Estimates are that in 1972, 53.4 percent of Texans opposed, versus 35.4 percent who favored a woman's right to choose an abortion. Uslaner and Weber, 218.
78. Southern Baptist Convention, *1971 Annual*, 72.
79. "Readers Back More Liberal Abortion Law," *Baptist Standard* (23 April 1969); and "Abortion Decision: A Death Blow?" *Christianity Today* (16 February 1973): 48.
80. Granberg, "Abortion Activists"; and Granberg and Granberg, 254-58.
81. Sydney E. Ahlstrom, *A Religious History of the American People* (New Haven: Yale University Press, 1972): 1079-96.
82. Baptist General Convention of Texas, *1974 Annual*, 25.
83. Baptist General Convention of Texas, *1976 Annual*, 65.
84. Baptist General Convention of Texas, *1980 Annual*, 72.
85. Southern Baptist Convention, *1984 Annual*, 65.
86. For moderate Baptist positions, see Paul D. Simmons, "The 'Human' as a Problem in Bioethics," *Review and Expositor* 78 (Winter 1981): 91-108; and the numerous unpublished essays by Joe Barnhart of North Texas State University.
87. Martha Hume, "Abortion in Texas," *Texas Monthly* 2 (March 1974): 55-68, esp. 65-68.
88. Granberg, "Abortion Activists," 161-63; and Donald Granberg and Beth Wellman Granberg, "Pro-life Versus Pro-choice: Another Look at the Abortion Controversy in the U.S.," *Sociology and Social Research* 65 (1981): 424-34.
89. Hume, 55-68; and Baptist General Convention of Texas, *1974 Annual*, 25.
90. Glenn Miller, "Church and State," in *Encyclopedia of the American Religious Experience*, vol. III, ed. Charles H. Lippy and Peter W. Williams (New York: Scribner's, 1988), 1388-89.

Lectures and participants

Humanities Perspectives on Medical Science and Technology in Texas: Personal Choices and Community Values Concerning Birth, Life, and Death

Nacogdoches
Literature and Medicine: Illness from the Patient's Point of View
By **Anne Hudson Jones**, Ph.D., Associate Professor of Literature and Medicine, Institute for the Medical Humanities (IMH), The University of Texas Medical Branch at Galveston (UTMB)
Discussant: **Jim E. Towns**, Ph.D., Professor, Department of Communication, Stephen F. Austin State University
Moderator: **Barbara Carr**, Ph.D., Associate Professor, Department of English and Philosophy, Stephen F. Austin State University

Corpus Christi
Life History, Oral History, and Case History: The Story of Eldrewey Stearns, Integration Leader
By **Thomas R. Cole**, Ph.D., Assistant Professor of History and Medicine, IMH, UTMB
Respondent: **Joe Frantz**, Ph.D., Turnbull Professor of History, College of Arts and Humanities, Corpus Christi State University
Moderator: **Michael J. Clayborne**, Attorney-at-Law, Corpus Christi

Beaumont
"Babe" Didrikson Zaharias: Her Personal and Public Battle with Cancer
By **Susan E. Cayleff**, Ph.D., Assistant Professor of History and Medicine, IMH, UTMB
Respondent: Dr. **Belle Mead Holm**, Professor, Department of Health, Physical Education, and Dance, Lamar University
Moderator: **Ralph Wooster**, Professor of History, Lamar University

Fort Worth
Caring for Congenitally Handicapped Newborns
By **Ronald A. Carson**, Ph.D., Kempner Professor and Director, IMH, UTMB
Respondents: **Stephen Kurachek**, M.D., Medical Director, Pediatric Intensive Care, Cook Children's and Fort Worth Children's Hospitals;

and **Ted Klein**, Ph.D., Professor, Department of Philosophy, Texas Christian University
Introduction by: **Manfred G. Reinecke**, Ph.D., Professor of Chemistry and Chairman, Health Professions Advisory Committee, Texas Christian University

Galveston
The 1988 Edgar H. and Lillye Mae Vaughn Lecture in Medical Philosophy and Morality and UTMB Department of Internal Medicine Grand Rounds:
What Does Life Support Support?
By **Albert R. Jonsen**, Ph.D., Professor of Ethics in Medicine, University of California at San Francisco School of Medicine

Georgetown
Life and Death Choices: The Patient's Rights
By **William J. Winslade**, Ph.D., J.D., Associate Professor of Medical Jurisprudence and Psychiatry, IMH, UTMB
Respondent: Justice **Bob Gammage**, Court of Appeals, Third Supreme Judicial District of Texas, Austin
Moderator: **G. Benjamin Oliver**, Dean, Brown College of Arts and Sciences, Southwestern University

San Angelo
Death with Dignity: Patients' Rights and the Texas Hospice Movement
By **Rebecca Dresser**, J.D., Assistant Professor, Center for Ethics, Medicine, and Public Issues, Baylor College of Medicine, Houston
Respondents: **John Hunt**, M.D., Medical Director, Hospice of San Angelo, and oncologist in private practice; and **Kenneth Stewart**, Ph.D., Associate Professor of Sociology, and Head, Department of Psychology and Sociology, Angelo State University
Moderator: **Judithe Hanover Zenter**, R.N., Ph.D., Associate Professor of Nursing, Angelo State University, and Hospice Consultant-Thanatologist

Edinburg
Death and Age: A Natural Connection?
By **Sally A. Gadow**, Ph.D., Associate Professor of Philosophy, IMH, UTMB
Respondent and Moderator: **Rumaldo Juarez**, Chairman, Department of Sociology, Pan American University

Denton
In Whose Image? Ethical Issues in Genetic Engineering
By **Thomas H. Murray**, Ph.D., Associate Professor of Medicine and

149

Public Policy, IMH, UTMB
Respondent: **Pete A. Y. Gunter**, Ph.D., Department of Philosophy, North Texas State University
Moderator: **Don W. Smith**, Ph.D., Department of Biology, North Texas State University

Galveston
A Glimpse at Galveston's Medical Past, 1836–1885
By **Chester R. Burns**, M.D., Ph.D., James Wade Rockwell Professor of the History of Medicine, IMH, UTMB
Discussants: **William C. Levin**, M.D., President, UTMB; and **M. L. Ross**, M.D., Founding Chairman of the Department of Family Medicine, UTMB, and former mayor, Galveston, Texas
Moderator: **William J. Winslade**, Ph.D., J.D, Associate Professor, IMH, UTMB

Lubbock
Abortion in Texas: Legal Enactments, Religious Traditions, and Social Hegemony
By **Harold Y. Vanderpool**, Ph.D., Th.M., Associate Professor of the History and Philosophy of Medicine, IMH, UTMB
Respondent: Professor **Daniel J. Benson**, School of Law, Texas Tech University
Moderator: Dr. **Tom McGovern**, Department of Psychiatry, Texas Tech University Health Science Center

Texas Medical Humanists

The following is a partial list of scholars, clinicians, and others in Texas who have special interests in the medical humanities. One purpose of assembling this list is to stimulate communication among persons interested in the medical humanities. Another purpose is to help local communities identify medical humanists for future teaching, public lectures, or community service. The list was compiled from the current membership list of the Society for Health and Human Values, from the files of the Texas Committee for the Humanities and the Institute for the Medical Humanities, from responses to a widely distributed letter that sought to identify medical humanists in Texas, and from personal communications. It is likely, however, other interested persons should be included in this list. Please submit names that should be included in future directories to William J. Winslade, Institute for the Medical Humanities, University of Texas Medical Branch, Galveston, Texas 77550.

Daniel C. Allensworth, M.D.
Internal Medicine
Medical Director, Heart Station
John Sealy Towers 8D, B-40
University of Texas Medical Branch
Galveston, TX 77550

Robert Abzug, Ph.D.
Department of History
University of Texas at Austin
Austin, TX 78712

Eric Avery, M.D.
Box 191
San Ignacio, TX 78067

William R. Baldwin, O.D., Ph.D.
Dean of Optometry
University of Houston—University Park
4800 Calhoun Road
Houston, TX 77004

Daniel Benson, J.D.
Law School
Texas Tech University
Lubbock, TX 79409

Gene V. Boisaubin, Jr., M.D.
Department of Medicine
Baylor College of Medicine
One Baylor Plaza
Houston, TX 77030

George N. Boyd, Ph.D.
Department of Religion
Trinity University
715 Stadium Drive
San Antonio, TX 78284

James O. Breeden, Ph.D.
Department of History
Southern Methodist University
Dallas, TX 75275

Baruch Brody, Ph.D.
Department of Community Medicine
Center for Ethics, Medicine, and Public Issues
Baylor College of Medicine
One Baylor Plaza
Houston, TX 77030

D. Clayton Brown, Ph.D.
Professor of History
Texas Christian University
P. O. Box 32888
Fort Worth, TX 76129

Chester R. Burns, M.D., Ph.D.
James Wade Rockwell Professor of the History of Medicine
Institute for the Medical Humanities
University of Texas Medical Branch
Galveston, TX 77550

James G. Burrow, Ph.D.
Department of History
Abilene Christian College
Abilene, TX 79699

Ronald A. Carson, Ph.D.
Kempner Professor and Director
Institute for the Medical Humanities
University of Texas Medical Branch
Galveston, TX 77559

James B. Carter, M.D.
2802 Northwood Road
Austin, TX 78703

Thomas R. Cole, Ph.D.
Institute for the Medical Humanities
University of Texas Medical Branch
Galveston, TX 77550

William R. Cozart, Ph.D.
Professor of English
Stephen F. Austin State University
P. O. Box 1300 F, SFA Station
Nacogdoches, TX 75962

Al Crosby, Ph.D.
Department of History
University of Texas at Austin
Austin, TX 78712

Eleanor Crowder, Ph.D.
The University of Texas School of Nursing
1700 Red River
Austin, TX 78701

Kathryn J. Dolan, Ph.D.
Assistant Professor of Medical Humanities
Department of Medical Humanities
Texas College of Osteopathic Medicine
Camp Bowie at Montgomery
Fort Worth, TX 76107

John W. Douard, Ph.D.
Institute for the Medical Humanities
University of Texas Medical Branch
Galveston, TX 77550

Reverend Brian Donovan
Director
Rice TMC Catholic Center
1703 Bolsover
Houston, TX 77005

H. Tristram Engelhardt, Ph.D., M.D.
Department of Community Medicine
Center for Ethics, Medicine, and Public Issues
Baylor College of Medicine
One Baylor Plaza
Houston, TX 77030

George Q. Flynn, Ph.D.
Department of History
Texas Tech University
Box 4529
Lubbock, TX 79409

Daniel Foster, M.D.
Chairman of Internal Medicine
University of Texas at Dallas Health Science Center
5323 Harry Hines Blvd.
Dallas, TX 75275

Sally Gadow, Ph.D.
Institute for the Medical Humanities
University of Texas Medical Branch
Galveston, TX 77550

Clyde Gallehugh, D.O.
Chairman—Medical Humanities Department
Texas College of Osteopathic Medicine
Camp Bowie at Montgomery
Fort Worth, TX 76107

Mary M. Hale, Ph.D.
Department of Political Science
Texas Tech University
Box 4290
Lubbock, TX 79409

Kenneth W. Hamstra
Hamstra Enterprises, Inc.
5901 Blue Buff Road
Austin, TX 78724

David B. Hausman, Ph.D.
Chairman—Philosophy Department
Southern Methodist University
Dallas, TX 75275

Martha Highfield, R.N., M.N.S.C.
10739 Shannon Hills
Houston, TX 77099

Peggy Hildreth, M.D.
1419 Kingstree Lane
Houston, TX 77058

Reverend Nolan D. Holcomb
Campus Minister
University of Texas Medical Branch
Galveston, TX 77550

Gerald H. Holman, M.D.
P. O. Box 950
Amarillo, TX 79176

Paxton H. Howard, Jr., M.D.
Chief, Section of Infectious Disease
Scott and White Clinic
Temple, TX 76501

Gary W. Humble, J.D.
219 Alvarez Drive
El Paso, TX 79932-1403

Anne Hudson Jones, Ph.D.
Institute for the Medical Humanities
University of Texas Medical Branch
Galveston, TX 77550

James H. Jones, Ph.D.
Department of History
University of Houston
Houston, TX 77004

Patsy K. Keyser
3959 Calculus Drive
Dallas, TX 75244

Ted Klein, Ph.D.
Philosophy Department
Texas Christian University
Fort Worth, TX 76129

Lonnie D. Kliever, Ph.D.
Professor of Religious Studies
Department of Religious Studies
Southern Methodist University
Dallas, TX 75275

Ronica M. Kluge, M.D.
Department of Internal Medicine
4112 John Sealy Hospital E66
University of Texas Medical Branch
Galveston, TX 77550

Ellen Breckenridge Koch
5110 Patrick Henry Street
Bellaire, TX 77401

David Kronick, M.D.
The University of Texas Medical School at San Antonio
7703 Floyd Curl Drive
San Antonio, TX 78229

Harry S. Lipscomb, M.D.
Route 1, Box 41 A
Bryan, TX 77807

Jaclyn Low, O.T.
University of Texas School of Allied Health Sciences
University of Texas Medical Branch
Galveston, TX 77550

William F. May, Ph.D.
Cary M. Maguire University Professor of Ethics
Department of Religious Studies
Southern Methodist University
318 Dallas Hall
Dallas, TX 75275

Larry McCullough, Ph.D.
Department of Community Medicine
Center for Ethics, Medicine, and Public Issues
Baylor College of Medicine
One Baylor Plaza
Houston, TX 77030

John J. McDermott, Ph.D.
Distinguished Professor of Philosophy and Humanities and
    Professor and Head
Department of Humanities and Medicine
Texas A&M University
Department of Philosophy
College Station, TX 77843

John P. McGovern, M.D.
McGovern Allergy Clinic
6969 Brompton
Houston, TX 77025

Thomas F. McGovern, Ed.D.
Associate Professor
Department of Psychiatry
TTUHSC School of Medicine
Lubbock, TX 79430

Ellen More, Ph.D.
Institute for the Medical Humanities
University of Texas Medical Branch
Galveston, TX 77550

Richard Morgan, M.D.
Department of Internal Medicine and
    Department of Family and Community Medicine
Texas A&M University College of Medicine
College Station, TX 77843

Charles Morrissey, M.D.
Baylor College of Medicine
One Baylor Plaza
Houston, TX 77030

David Mumford, M.D.
Department of Obstetrics and Gynecology
Baylor College of Medicine
One Baylor Plaza
Houston, TX 77030

J. Robert Nelson, D.Theol.
Director
The Institute of Religion
Texas Medical Center
P.O. Box 20569
Houston, TX 77225

William Nelson, Ph.D.
Department of Philosophy
University of Houston
Houston, TX 77004

Charles Ogilvie, D.O.
Department of Medical Humanities
Texas College of Osteopathy
Camp Bowie at Montgomery
Fort Worth, TX 76107

Leonard G. Paul, M.D.
Chairman, Department of Family Medicine
University of Texas Health Science Center at San Antonio
7703 Floyd Curl Drive
San Antonio, TX 78284

Rex C. Peebles, Ph.D.
Social and Behavioral Sciences
Austin Community College
1201 Rio Grande
Austin, TX 78748

Henry S. Perkins, M.D.
Assistant Professor of Medicine
Consultant in Medical Ethics
Division of General Medicine
Department of Medicine
The University of Texas Health Science Center at San Antonio
7703 Floyd Curl Drive
San Antonio, TX 78284

James Campbell Quick, Ph.D.
Department of Management
Box 19088
The University of Texas at Arlington
Arlington, TX 76019

Robert E. Rakel, M.D.
Family Practice Center
5510 Greenbriar
Houston, TX 77005

Billy Reeves, M.D.
Professor
Department of Obstetrics/Gynecology
Texas Tech University Health Sciences Center
Regional Academic Health Center at El Paso
School of Medicine/Dept. of Obstetrics and Gynecology
4800 Alberta Avenue
El Paso, TX 79905

Stanley T. Reiser, M.D., Ph.D.
Program in Humanities and Technology in Medicine
P. O. Box 20708, Room 1.500
University of Texas Health Science Center at Houston
6431 Fannin Houston, TX 77025

John Robertson, J.D.
Law School
University of Texas
Austin, TX 78712

James O. Robinson, M.D.
Professor of Surgery
University of Texas Health Science Center at Dallas
Surgery Department E7, 126
5323 Harry Hines Blvd.
Dallas, TX 75235

Patrick Romanell, Ph.D.
H. Y. Benedict Professor of Philosophy
The University of Texas at El Paso
El Paso, TX 79968

Thomas Satre, Ph.D.
Philosophy Program Coordinator
Professor of Philosophy
Sam Houston State University
Huntsville, TX 77341

Megan Seaholm, Ph.D.
Research Associate
Centennial History Project J05
University of Texas Medical Branch
Galveston, TX 77550

Melvyn H. Schreiber, M.D.
Professor and Chairman of Radiology
McCullough Building G09
University of Texas Medical Branch
Galveston, TX 77550

Linda S. Scheirton, M.A., R.D.H.
Dental Hygiene Education
University of Texas Health Science Center at San Antonio
7703 Floyd Curl Drive
San Antonio, TX 78284

Reverend W. Francis Schorp
Department of Philosophy
St. Mary's University
San Antonio, TX 78284

John Slore, Ph.D.
Southwestern University
Box 6200
Georgetown, TX 78626

Donnie J. Self, Ph.D.
Department of Humanities in Medicine
Texas A&M University College of Medicine
164 Medical Sciences Building
College Station, TX 77843

Earl Shelp, Ph.D.
Executive Director
Foundation for Interfaith Research and Ministry
Box 20392
Houston, TX 77225

Edgar B. Smith, M.D.
Professor and Chairman
Department of Dermatology
Clinical Sciences Building G83
University of Texas Medical Branch
Galveston, TX 77550

Frederick J. Streng, Ph.D.
Professor of Religious Studies
Southern Methodist University
Dallas, TX 75275

John Swann, Ph.D.
Research Associate
Centennial History Project
University of Texas Medical Branch
Galveston, TX 77550

Laurence Tancredi, M.D., J.D.
Health Law Program
School of Public Health Building
Suite 901
1200 Herman Pressler Drive
Houston, TX 77030

Fred M. Taylor, M.D.
810 Alhambra
Sugarland, TX 77478

Terry Jay Thompson
Associate Minister
St. Paul's United Methodist Church
5501 South Main Street
Houston, TX 77004

Kay Toombs
1226 Ashleman
Waco, TX 76705

Courtney Townsend, Jr., M.D.
Professor of Surgery
Department of Surgery
6136 John Sealy Hospital E27
University of Texas Medical Branch
Galveston, TX 77550

Poldi Ann Tschirch, R.N.
#4 Tiki Circle
Galveston, TX 77551

Albert Van Helden, Ph.D.
Department of History
Rice University
P. O. Box 1892
Houston, TX 77251

Harold V. Vanderpool, Ph.D.
Institute for the Medical Humanities
University of Texas Medical Branch
Galveston, TX 77550

John M. Wallace, M.D.
Professor of Internal Medicine
5a John Sealy Hospital E91
University of Texas Medical Branch
Galveston, TX 77550

Jack Weir, Ph.D.
Professor of Philosophy
Hardin-Simmons University
Box 1234
HUS Station
Abilene, TX 79698

Gary B. Weiss, M.D.
Bay Area Oncology—Hematology
450 Blossom Street
Webster, TX 77598

Elizabeth Borst White
Houston Academy of Medicine
Texas Medical Center Library
1133 M. D. Anderson Blvd.
Houston, TX 77030

Joseph M. White, M.D.
Department of Medical Education
St. Paul's Hospital
5909 Harry Hines Blvd.
Dallas, TX 75235

Mary Winkler, Ph.D.
Institute for the Medical Humanities
University of Texas Medical Branch
Galveston, TX 77550

William J. Winslade, Ph.D., J.D.
Institute for the Medical Humanities
University of Texas Medical Branch
Galveston, TX 77550

Selected Bibliography

Listed below are some of the books written or edited by Texas Medical Humanists. Recently published books in the medical humanities are reviewed in *Medical Humanities Review*, published twice a year by the Institute for the Medical Humanities. In addition, many persons listed in the Directory of Texas Medical Humanists have written articles and essays in the medical humanities.

1. Brody, Baruch, *Life and Death Decision Making*. New York: Oxford University Press, 1988.
2. Bulger, Roger J., ed., *In Search of the Modern Hippocrates*. Iowa City: University of Iowa Press, 1987.
3. Cole, Thomas R. and Gadow, Sally, eds. *What Does It Mean to Grow Old?: Reflections from the Humanities*. Durham: Duke University Press, 1986.
4. Engelhardt, H. Tristram, Jr., *The Foundations of Bioethics*. New York: Oxford University Press, 1986.
5. Jones, Anne Hudson, ed., *Images of Nurses: Perspectives from History, Art, and Literature*. Philadelphia: University of Pennsylvania Press, 1988.
6. Jonsen, A., Siegler, M. and Winslade, W. J., *Clinical Ethics*. 2d ed. New York: Macmillan, 1986.
7. Kliever, Lonnie D., ed., *Dax's Case*. Dallas: Southern Methodist University Press, 1989.
8. May, William F., *The Physician's Covenant*. Philadelphia: Westminster Press, 1983.
9. McDermott, John J., *Streams of Experience*. Amherst: The University of Massachusetts Press, 1986.
10. Reiser, Stanley Joel, *Medicine and the Reign of Technology*. New York: Cambridge University Press, 1978.
11. Reiser, Stanley Joel and Anbar, Michael, eds., *The Machine at the Bedside*. New York: Cambridge University Press, 1985.
12. Robertson, John A., *The Rights of the Critically Ill*. Cambridge: Ballinger Publishing Company, 1983.
13. Shelp, Earl, *Born To Die*. New York: The Free Press, 1986.
14. Winslade, William J. and Ross, Judith Wilson, *Choosing Life or Death*. New York: The Free Press, 1986.

DATE DUE

NOV 1 6 1991			